The Monastic Cloister *of* My Heart

Poetic Reflections and Prayers from the Edge of Life

GERARD THOMAS STRAUB

Published by:

Pax et Bonum Communications

VERO BEACH, FLORIDA

© 2026 Pax et Bonum Communications, Inc.

ISBN-13: 979-8-9860888-5-3
Ebook: 979-8-9860888-6-0

Edited by
Carol Killman Rosenberg

Cover & interior design by
Gary A. Rosenberg

www.thebookcouple.com

Cover painting by
Lewis Williams

Printed in the United States of America

*The publication of this book was made possible
by the financial support of*

Martanne Allman

Joe Berberich

Fr. Bob Bonnot

George Caddy

Deborah Chrzanowski

Steve Jones

Lisa & John Juriga

Teresa Madden

June L. Mumme

Patti Normile

Christine Osterman

Melanie Sanchez-Jones

Jane & Mike Skiba

Willem Tensen

Timothy Welch

Other Books by Gerard Thomas Straub

Salvation for Sale

Dear Kate (a novel)

The Sun & Moon Over Assisi

When Did I See You Hungry?
(photo/essay)

Thoughts of a Blind Beggar

Hidden in the Rubble

The Loneliness and Longing
of Saint Francis

The Sunrise of the Soul

A Journey to Meekness

Reading Thomas Merton and
Longing for God in Haiti

The Cross of Love,
The Pain of Poverty

Looking In, Looking Out

Films by Gerard Thomas Straub

We Have a Table for Four Ready

Room Enough for Joy

Glidepath to Recovery

When Did I See You Hungry?

Embracing the Leper

Holy Pictures

Rescue Me

Endless Exodus

Poverty and Prayer

The Patience of a Saint

Where Love Is

The Faces of Poverty

Room at the Inn

The Narrow Path

The Fragrant Spirit of Life

Poverty and Prayer II

A Distressing Disguise

Cathedrals of the Poor

Mud Pies & Kites

We Anoint Their Wounds

The Wings of Love

The Smile of a Sick Child

Rooted in Love

Silenzio

The Loneliness and Longing
of St. Francis of Assisi

In June 2025, when this book was still very much a work in progress, I sent it to a friend, a very special friend I have known for twenty-five years and with whom I can say anything. He knows more about me than anyone else. He brightens even my darkest days. He wrote the foreword to my book *Reading Thomas Merton and Longing for God in Haiti*. He read about eighty pages of an early draft of this book and wrote the following:

> *"I feel water-boarded by the authenticity of your sacred life*
> *from which these words emerge and flow out from you.*
> *To read your 'word' with knowledge of your living them is*
> *like drowning within a faith I do not know; even faintly*
> *comprehending this faith of yours is a frightening experience."*

> —JONATHAN MONTALDO,
> *Thomas Merton's Dialogues with Silence*
> *The Intimate Merton*

Opening Prayer

"Lord and Master of my life, do not give me a spirit of sloth,
idle curiosity, love of power and useless chatter.
Rather impart to me your servant a spirit of chastity,
humility, endurance, and love.
Yes, Lord and King, grant me to see my own faults and not
to condemn my brother; for you are blessed to the ages
of ages. Amen."

—St. Ephrem the Syrian
"The Greek Writings Attributed to Saint Ephrem the Syrian"
by Ephrem Lash
found in *Abba: The Tradition of the Orthodox in the West*
(Crestwood, NY: St. Vladimir's Seminary Press, 2003, page 82)

This humble book
mostly deals with
the spiritual side
of my twenty-five-year journey
with the poor.

In this book,
when I use the word "monk,"
it means more than male monks,
and includes women
living as cloistered nuns,
as well as all laypeople
living the essence of cenobitic life
without walls or a community . . .
like me.

Dedicated to

All the Children
of the
Santa Chiara Children's Center and Academy
in Port-au-Prince, Haiti

Photograph by Orlane Alexandré

Smiles easily grace my face
when I am hanging out with the kids.
They have given me a new life;
my life would be empty without them.
We are trying our best to give them
hope and tools for a better future.

"Right at the depth of the human condition,
lies the longing for presence,
the silent desire for communion.
Let us never forget this simple desire for God
is already the beginning of faith."

—Br. Roger Schutz, Prior of Taizé

"The word vocation comes from the Latin *vocare*, to call,
and means the work a man is called to by God.
There are all different kinds of voices calling you
to all different kinds of work,
and the problem is to find out which is
the voice of God rather than of society . . .
The place God calls you to is the place where
your deep gladness and the world's deep hunger meet."

—Frederick Buechner

Contents

Foreword

I am honored to offer a personal note to Gerry Staub's latest book, *The Monastic Cloister of My Heart*. In his prose poems, we are gifted with a lifetime of change and transformation to help us all on our own journeys.

I hope you are aware of John Henry Newman's brilliant observation: "To live is to change, and to be perfect is to have changed often." Gerry has changed often, and I suspect he is ever ready to change more and more.

I attended a Calvin College January Series lecture in Grand Rapids some years ago where Gerry spoke and shared clips from his many documentaries on poverty all over the world. It was an extraordinarily moving presentation. A few years later, Gerry was invited by the Paulist Fathers to be the presenter for the Fr. Gallagher Memorial Lecture at St. Andrew Cathedral in Grand Rapids, Michigan. The gripping story of his life in Haiti amidst barbaric gang violence, as well as the stunning footage from his remarkable films set in Uganda and Haiti, were seared into the audience's memory. I was delighted to offer Gerry my small guest room during his stay.

We found we had many similar mentors in Thomas Merton, Dorothy Day, John Dear, Dom Helder Camara, Oscar Romero, John XXIII, and especially St. Francis of Assisi and St. Clare. We also enjoyed similar interests in Orthodox icons and the artwork of Rembrandt, Rouault, Van Gogh, John August Swanson, and many others. Over and over again, over Starbucks coffees, we talked about spirituality, theology, mysticism, monasticism, church history, and the great moral issues of our day: poverty, world hunger, war, violence, nuclear weapons, luxury, avarice, the unfair and immoral distribution of wealth by both democratic and communist countries, and a capitalism distorted by propaganda and the super-rich.

Since then, I have become a true friend and faithful reader of his daily *Haiti Journal*. I am sure you also will find Gerry a dear friend and mentor,

"

a trustworthy guide, and a profound searcher for the good, the true, the beautiful, and the One.

Like it or not, believe it or not, accept it or not, our true home is in God. And God's true home is in each of us, God's beloved.

The Monastic Cloister of My Heart will delight you with love—unconditional love, nonviolent love, and preexistent love that existed before the physical and material world came to be.

—Fr. Paul Milanowski, retired priest of the
Catholic Diocese of Grand Rapids

Note: All Gerry's heart-wrenching documentaries are available for free, without downloading, at www.PaxetBonumComm.org.

Prologue:
I Need a Break

I need to just sit in silence.
To walk in nature.
To breathe deeply.
To read a book.
And not feel guilty
because I needed to be doing
    something
more important.
I never took the time
after battling Covid-19,
which nearly took my life,
to really rest and reflect,
to pray deeply.
While I love the kids
I serve,
I need a little break
from them.
I need a break
from the tensions
of this stressful work
a break
from the worry
about money
a break
from the complexity
of downsizing
a break
from the chaos and violence
a break
from the endless suffering
and insurmountable need.
I'd love to be flying
to Assisi
but Hutchinson Island
off the coast of
Fort Pierce, Florida
will do.
I depart tomorrow.
I need your prayers
for wisdom and guidance
as we face
an uncertain future
during these
troubling times.
There are days
I want to
stop . . .
to leave Haiti

but deep down
in my soul
I know
I can't.
I need a little
alone time

to reflect and
recharge.
I need to come apart
in order not
to fall apart.

Gerry Straub
July 31, 2020
Feast of St. Ignatius Loyola

On October 9, 2025, as I was reviewing this manuscript before sending it to the editor, I came across a word file titled "I need a break." I could not imagine what was in the file. I was surprised by the contents of the one page that foreshadowed the exile needed to write this book.

I Need a Break was, in essence, a prayer of petition.

In the following few pages, you will read how late in 2024 I was forced into exile by the violence in Haiti, which had reached unimaginable heights of barbarity. From January 2024 through September 2025, over 9,200 Haitians had been killed. By late 2025, the gangs controlled 90 percent of Port-au-Prince.

I was very upset by being separated from my kids in Haiti. I founded and operated a home for abandoned and abused kids in a slum in Port-au-Prince in May 2015. Since then, I spent 70 percent of my time in Haiti. Haiti had become my home. I traveled between Haiti and Florida every month. Suddenly in October 2024, flights to Haiti were banned. I felt lonely, lost, and isolated, cut off from the kids I loved.

On October 9, 2025, I felt that my exile was an unexpected answer to a prayer request for a break. I would not have taken a break . . . so, the break came to me. It has been painful. But necessary.

Within an hour of finding the file, a priest friend sent me a meditation penned by Henri Nouwen:

Somewhere we know that without a lonely place, our lives are in danger. Somewhere we know that without silence, words lose their meaning; that without listening, speaking no longer heals; that without distance, closeness cannot cure. Somewhere we know that without a solitary place, our actions quickly become empty gestures. The careful balance between silence and words, withdrawal and involvement, distance and closeness, solitude and community forms the basis of the spiritual life and should therefore be the subject of our most personal attention.

Rainer Marie Rilke wrote:

> *Now you must go out into your heart*
> *as on a vast plain. Now*
> *the immense loneliness begins . . .*

The spiritual life is a long journey, a pilgrimage to transformation in which we travel through our struggles, our sufferings, our setbacks. It seems the soul must weep to grow. Tears and laughter mingle together as we make our way into a new life. In our darkness, we find a flicker of light, which, when protected and nurtured, becomes illumination . . . and obstacles become opportunities to go deeper.

Prelude:
Living in Exile

This book was written in exile, far from where my heart was. I longed to return to the slums and chaos of Port-au-Prince, Haiti. After spending fifteen years making documentary films on global poverty, filming in the worst slums in eleven of the poorest nations on earth, I decided to put down my cameras and to intentionally live with the poor in Haiti. I have essentially lived in Haiti since 2015. Five years earlier, I had filmed the aftermath of the horrific earthquake in Haiti that killed over 300,000 people and left more than a million people homeless. I opened a home for abandoned and abused children called the Santa Chiara Children's Center. Since its opening, I have spent three weeks a month in Port-au-Prince and a week in America. The center is in a deeply impoverished area not far from the largest, most violent slum in the city. We have no running water. Most of my neighbors have no indoor plumbing and have electricity for only a few hours a day.

Haiti has a long history of violence. Over the last ten years in Haiti, I have witnessed waves of intense violence. My life was threatened on a few occasions. But starting in the summer of 2023—two years after the assassination of President Jovenel Moïse in his own bed—the gangs have controlled Port-au-Prince during a tsunami of barbaric violence, including beheading or setting people on fire.

By March 2024, the gangs were in control of about 80 percent of Port-au-Prince, and the situation was so volatile that the U.S. Embassy, which was closed due to the violence, arranged for American citizens, including me, to be evacuated by the U.S. Marines by helicopter. Marines drove us from the embassy to a field in an armored vehicle. The field was surrounded by dozens of Marines with machine guns. It was a frightening experience. We were flown to Santo Domingo in the Dominican Republic;

the next day I caught a flight back to Florida. I was able to return to Port-au-Prince a few months later. After landing in Haiti, I was met by two Haitian National Police officers wearing bullet-proof vests and carrying machine guns; they drove me home to the Santa Chiara Children's Center. For the rest of the year, they accompanied me anywhere I went in the city. One officer also came with me on my early morning walks . . . until he said it was no longer safe to leave Santa Chiara. It was very common to hear gunfire at night.

In 2024, more than 5,600 people were killed by the gangs, including women, children, and the elderly. No one was immune from the violence, including nuns, priests, and doctors. In October 2024, I was in Florida for two weeks to handle administrative duties. I was about to return to Port-au-Prince, when my security team advised me to wait a few weeks before returning, as they could not guarantee they could transport me safely from the airport to Santa Chiara. In November 2024, a few weeks after a brilliant, kind, and compassionate surgeon operated on one my kids, she was shot in the head by a gang member after leaving her father's clinic.

In late November 2024, the gangs shot at American passenger jets landing in or taking off from Port-au-Prince. Bullets penetrated two planes, slightly injuring one flight attendant. All flights from the United States to Haiti were canceled. Commercial flights would not be restored until . . . if at all. And so began my forced exile from Haiti.

The violence accelerated in 2025, as the gangs moved out beyond Port-au-Prince. During the first nine months of 2025, another 3,600 Haitians were slaughtered. The gangs swept through neighborhoods and set homes on fire . . . homes that were often not more than shacks . . . forcing families to flee with only what they could carry. Between January 2024 and September 2025, 1.4 million Haitians were forced from their homes as the gangs set fire to entire neighborhoods; people fled with what they wore and could carry. At least 1,000 schools have been closed, leaving 200,000 kids without an education. Without mercy or concern, the gangs ransacked and torched many hospitals. Only 28 percent of in-patient healthcare facilities nationwide are fully operational.

In late February 2025, a gang member took a three-month-old infant from a mother who was breastfeeding her child. The gang member then did the unthinkable: he tossed the infant in a fire the gangs had started. The mother was so hysterical that she died within hours. In late October 2025, the United Nations said that since the beginning of 2022, over 16,000 Haitians had been killed by gang violence. Insanity. Most people in Port-au-Prince live in a perpetual state of uncertainty, chaos, and fear.

In early September 2025, the FAA extended the ban on flights to Haiti until March 2026, and I have been forced to live in exile in Florida. My heart aches to return to my home in Haiti. Unexpectedly, I had time to write . . . *more deeply from my heart.*

This is a new form of writing for me. For ten years much of my writing was confined to my daily Journals from Haiti, detailing the ups and downs of essentially living in a war zone. I punctuated my documentation of the raw reality of slum life with spiritual reflections. I also shared the heartbreaking lives of some of the children before they had entered Santa Chiara, as well as the death of two of my kids. Between 2022 and 2024, I did manage to write three books, including, *Reading Thomas Merton and Longing for God in Haiti.* In the early months of my exile, I finished and published an epic book, *The Cross of Love, The Pain of Poverty,* which focused on my fifteen years of filming global poverty and ten years of living with the poor in Port-au-Prince, Haiti, where, as I've mentioned, I founded an orphanage named the Santa Chiara Children's Center and Academy.

With *The Monastic Cloister of My Heart,* I explored a new style of expression: prose poetry. I began occasionally sharing a poetic reflection in my Haiti Journal, which I routinely send to about 200 of the donors who supported my humble ministry in Haiti. I was surprised how well they were received. They were simple, clear, and mostly short. They invited the reader to read more slowly. As the collection of reflections grew, I began seeing a book emerge. I liked seeing all the white space on each page, which was more conducive in prompting meditative space for the reader.

Over the last twenty years, I have written at least a dozen manuscripts that were never published; some were never submitted to a publisher. I was continuously writing . . . *for my own personal salvation.* During my prolonged forced exile, I began reading all those manuscripts. Whenever I found a gem among the onslaught of words, I imagined how to change the prose into a poetic style. I felt the reformatted text was more impactful. I loved the process of literary recycling. I also saw more clearly my own spiritual journey, with all its ups and downs, all its mistakes and dead-end streets, and I saw how it all worked together to get me where I am today. I also began writing poetic expressions of my own spiritual struggles and epiphanies.

To be clear, I am not a poet. I only admit to having a poetic instinct. My scripts for my documentary films are closer to poetry than prose; they are simple, clear, and sparse. My books—especially *The Sun & Moon Over Assisi, Reading Thomas Merton and Longing for God in Haiti,* and *The Cross of Love, The Pain of Poverty*—were years in the making and were huge struggles to bring to fruition . . . and they were too long for a nonstop work culture where reading has largely been replaced by texting, podcasts, and social media.

The Monastic Cloister of My Heart is contemplative in spirit and hopefully draws you into a sense of stillness and silence as it awakens your contemplative heart . . . a page at a time. Go slowly and reflectively.

Introduction: Living in Humility and Simplicity

> *"Your life is shaped by the end you live for.*
> *You are made in the image of what you desire."*
>
> —Thomas Merton, Thoughts in Solitude

I think of myself as a monk without a monastery. I always wear a black, brimless cap that makes me look like a monk. I almost always wear black shirts. I am drawn to monks, monks of all faiths, but especially Catholic monks. I was reading Thomas Merton, the most famous Catholic monk of the last hundred years, even when I considered myself an atheist. I spent years writing a book about Merton and his influence on my life; titled *Reading Thomas Merton and Longing for God in Haiti,* it was published in 2023.

Back in my atheist days, I once briefly lived in a small village in Upstate New York that was the home of an Orthodox Christian monastery. I spent much of my time at the monastery. I talked with the monks and even volunteered to help them make sausages, which they sold to markets in neighboring towns. The monks called me Brother Hollywood because I once was a Hollywood television producer—back then I lived a very un-monk-like life. It was my time with Orthodox monks that cultivated my love of icons and the liturgy of St. John Chrysostom. I also once spent a week at a Benedictine monastery in New Mexico and another week at Trappist monastery in Kentucky, which had been the monastic home of Thomas Merton.

To think of myself as a monk is odd because besides being the "father" of more than fifty abandoned kids in Haiti, I also have been married (*more than once!*)—and I am not very comfortable with much of Catholicism even though it is my spiritual home. The celebrated Japanese Catholic novelist, Shusaku Endo, wrote: "There were many times when I felt I wanted to get rid of my Catholicism, but I was finally unable to do so. It is not just that I did not throw it off, but that I was unable to throw it off. The reason for this must be that it had become a part of me after all." Oh God, I know that feeling. I too could not let go of the faith of my youth, even after outgrowing it. It seems my brain was wired for Catholicism. But I ignore much of the dogmatic side of Catholicism and am deeply drawn to the mystical expression of the faith and its sincere concern about social justice and peace.

Bede Griffiths put it best: "If Christianity cannot recover its mystical tradition and teach it, it should just fold up and go out of business." He was a Camaldolese Benedictine monk, hermit, and priest who lived in ashrams in the south of India; by the end of his life, he was also known as Swami Dayananda ("bliss of compassion"). The mystics of all faiths are my spiritual friends. I guess I am an ecumenical monk.

Yet despite my attraction to monasticism, I am planted in the world . . . in the mud and gutters of the peripheries of earth. Most of the last twenty-five years of my life have been spent in the massive slums of the poorest nations on earth. St. Francis claimed the world was his cloister. I echo that attitude. Still, at times, I want to withdraw to a mountainside cave the way St. Francis regularly did. I could turn my apartment into a cave by simply unplugging from the internet and cable television. But ignoring the chaos and suffering of the world will not make it go away. A free-range monk without a monastery needs to be both a contemplative and an activist. He or she needs to nurture and heal his or her own soul and then help others find their own way of embracing the divinity within them. In the cloister of my own heart, I encounter the Origin of all, and I am moved to reach out to all I encounter on the margins and in mansions.

We have lost the beauty, sweetness, and wonder of life. We have become bitter and divided. We do not discuss and debate; we hate and eliminate. Political violence is on the rise. Life is so rich, so varied, yet for many, their view of life is very narrow and highly restricted. For most of my life, my view of life, of the world, was narrowly confined to the circles in which I lived and worked, primarily in New York City and Hollywood. It was not until I bumped into a medieval saint from Assisi who took me down the road to poverty that my eyes were opened to the vast and varied world beyond myself and my narrow interests. Whatever I thought about God and the world was so infinitesimally small it could have fit into one of my grandmother's thimbles, with room leftover.

In my far-flung travels, with camera in hand, I began to understand myself . . . and started to question all the "truths" and "certainties" I had held tightly. While filming the poor, I was searching for myself, trying to find some clarity to my stumbling, bumbling life. I was searching for my inner monk. My travels throughout Africa and South and Central America, as well as the Philippines, India, and Turkey, became a bridge to other cultures and religions. A journey outside oneself requires living in humility and simplicity.

Raimon Panikkar (1918–2010) was a Catholic priest and the author of more than forty-five books who specialized in comparative religion. By merging Hindu and Buddhist thought with Christianity, Panikkar became a leader of interreligious dialogue. St. Francis of Assisi pioneered interreligious dialogue by meeting with the Muslim sultan in a futile attempt to end the Crusades. Raimon Panikkar suggested that while interreligious dialogue is important, it needs to be coupled with intrareligious dialogue within yourself. In time, my soul became a temple of intrareligious dialogue. I treasure my Jewish and Muslim friends . . . and continue to learn from them.

Raimundo Panikkar believed there was a monastic archetype, or a contemplative dimension innate in every human being. I agree. Without a contemplative dimension, my work in Haiti never would have lasted ten years. I had to, for the sake of survival, sprinkle time for stillness and silence into every month, to come apart and focus on my inner life. Even during the chaos and violence of a day in Haiti, I would retreat to my office and sit in silence for at least five minutes. I would look out my window at the beauty of the mountainous horizon, which filled me with wonder.

Without fully realizing it, we often pretend to be who we are not, which means we play roles rather than simply being ourselves. I played the role of a television producer for many years, while loathing the shows I produced, as well as the industry that manufactured mindless, often crass entertainment that were weapons of mass distraction from what is essential. The shows I produced were vehicles to promote consumerism. Our "art" was used as vehicle to get viewers to shop, often by creating a need for something we did not need.

It has been at least thirty-five years since I last produced a network television show. It took a long time to begin stripping away who I had been and ever so slowly began to operate out of a purity of heart. Writing about St. Francis of Assisi was motivated simply by wanting to learn how to live differently. I had not planned to pursue publishing a book about the saint. I was not pretending to be a scholar of Franciscanism. I was sincerely trying to enter fully into the life of a person who took Christ so seriously that it transformed his being. I wanted transformation, not recognition.

I wrote a book that I wished I could have found, a book that was not clothed in dispassionate academics, but was as down to earth and fully human (heart, mind, and soul) as the saint himself. I wanted to know and understand the saint's love not just of the poor, but of poverty itself, which seemed crazy as we all need money and are too insecure to live by trusting in divine providence. We need to make plans. We need to know. We need certainty. Poverty certainly cannot be a path to knowledge, security, and certainty. Along the way, I saw that I learned more from my detractors than from my admirers. The book that I wrote, *The Sun & Moon Over Assisi*, was named the Best Spirituality Hardcover Book of the Year in 2001 by the Catholic Press Association. I have heard many stories from people who told me that reading the book changed their lives.

I am still learning to enjoy the banquet of life. I needed to live from my deepest being, which is something I frequently failed to do. But now, in the winter of my life, with my days growing shorter, I can look back and the seemingly crazy, impractical choices I made from the depths of my being were the most beneficial to me. Closing the door on commercial television production because I wanted to know about the little boy I once was who had the dream to be a Vincentian missionary priest taking the Gospel to China. It was, in the eyes of others, a ridiculous thing to do. Then, after fifteen years of filming poverty and speaking about poverty at more than 260 churches, high schools, and universities, I felt the pull to put the camera down and to live among the poor and serve kids in dire need. That was an even crazier idea.

The lesson in all this is clear: follow your heart. We hear that all the time, but few do it. We do not do it because of our deep-seated need for certainty and security. We are obsessed with certainty and security. Philosophy demands certainty. Religion should have a sense of insecurity and room for doubt, uncertainty, and even confusion. But we are too full of ourselves to live without certainty and security. We know the truth and we cling to it. We live in an artificial world we created that is far from the divinely created world where everything is in relationship with everything. Knowledge without love destroys you. Love without knowledge is merely sentimentalism. We need both knowledge and love without any separation.

Before you read this book further, put aside your worries and concerns and sit in peace for a few moments. Take a deep breath. Be still. Focus on your inner being. When you begin reading, go slowly. I suggest only reading one reflection at a time, pausing afterward for a few minutes of contemplation. Most of these reflections "came" to me in poetic form. This is good, because it naturally slows down the reading and allows you to focus more on each line. If a reflection does not speak to you, just move onto the next one.

I wish you peace.

Preamble:
A Living Film

On November 13, 2025, as I waited for a 3:00 pm call from Father John Dear during which he would record our "conversation" for his podcast, I was searching an old external manuscript for a film treatment on St. Francis of Assisi that I had written with John and the Franciscan priest and writer Murray Bodo. The film was titled Francesco. The epic film we dreamed of making in 2001 was never made; it was too costly. I came across the only printed copy of the film treatment a few months earlier, and I could not stop thinking about it. I was on the verge of reimagining it as a book. While my search of old external drives came up empty, I came across a file named "living film." I had no idea what was in the file, so I opened it to find out. The file consisted of the following:

At the conclusion of the Zoom "lecture" sponsored by the Trappist Monastery in South Carolina in early October 2020, the monk (and priest) in charge of the St. Francis Retreat Center at Mepkin Abbey said to me and all those attending the event: "Gerry, you've ceased making films and in your own way have become a living film as way of connecting people like ourselves to the suffering part of our own humanity and calling us to ask what we are we doing in our own lives. You are more of a monk than you give yourself credit for. Perhaps living with the poor is one of the deepest forms of prayer. Thank you for what you shared and the deeper level you've called us to."

Suddenly, "The Monastic Cloister of My Heart" was not such a far-fetched title.

PART ONE

Reflections

Suffused with Light

I called it an epiphany.
A fleeting epiphany.
It happened in
an empty church
in Rome.
I was not praying.
I was an atheist.
I was simply resting
in a silent, cool spot.

I opened a book
that was quietly sitting
on the bench.
I read Psalm 63.
It was about a soul
thirsting for God.
Suddenly, my dark
image of God
immediately was
suffused with light.

The notion of a harsh,
judging God
waiting for me
to slip up and
then condemn me
to burn
in the eternal place
called hell
was banished.

In its place,
a loving God
hugged me
and loved me
just as I am,
a very flawed
weak man
stumbling through
a meaningless life.

After that mysterious
moment
everything in my life
changed.
I began writing about
St. Francis of Assisi.
In time, I followed him
down poverty road
filming the poor
and marginalized
in some of the worst slums
on earth
and eventually
living with the poor
in Haiti.

A Very Lonely Road

St. Francis of Assisi
longed for God
beyond all measure.
His intense longing
took him to places
few had traveled to,
places deep within himself
and places far from Assisi.
On his journey to God
he traveled down
a very lonely road.

His soul longed for God
even in the night;
from early morning
and throughout the day,
with the sweet affection of Mary,
he kept watch,
looking and longing
for God
and God alone.

To long for God
is already
to experience,
albeit faintly,
the presence of God.
To experience
more and more of God
was all Francis wanted.
It is all
we need.

Icons of Holiness

Somewhere deep inside each of us, there is a desire to be holy. We can quibble about what being holy means, but essentially it means being really good . . . even when no one is watching. For a Christian, the essential meaning of holiness is more precise: it means being like Christ. The manifest goodness on full display in the lives of the saints grew out of love. Their love of God was so strong, so deep that their lives pulsated with God's love and goodness.

Saints are icons
of holiness.
Saints make holiness real;
they show us holiness
is possible.
Saints are also
fully human.
They make mistakes
and have their share
of failures.
They cry and they laugh.
They endure illnesses
and disappointments.
They fight long and hard
to overcome doubts and
    insecurities.
They often experience
rejection and scorn
from family and friends.

Saints struggle with
spiritual growth
as they attempt to follow
a path
they hope and pray
leads to God.
They are ordinary people
whose passion to emulate
the self-emptying love of Christ
is extraordinary.

Saints are flesh and blood,
not pious plastic statues.
They are not perfect,
but they allowed the love of
    Christ
to transform their
weaknesses and imperfections
into something beautiful.

The Human Face of Jesus

As I made my humble films on global and domestic poverty, I slowly learned to see the poor and the marginalized, the alcoholic, the drug addict, the mentally ill, and the homeless not as objects of pity and charity but as brothers and sisters with whom I am intimately related. The longer I walk with the poor, the more I see the need to put to death the idea of my own self-sufficiency. To think of myself as separate from God and all of creation, including the poor and the outcast, is an illusion.

St. Francis understood
we all are
the human face of Jesus;
he knew that
all of humanity comprises
the divine face.

God assumed flesh
and was born into a world of
oppression and persecution.
Can we ever grasp the reality
of the divine presence
dwelling in a depraved humanity
and that subsequently
every man, woman, and child
is uniquely precious,
equal and blessed,
all brothers and sisters?

Jesus is hungry and naked.
Yet we build and decorate
elaborate churches
in His name,
but do not feed or clothe Him.
Every day,
God comes to us
in a distressing disguise,
clothed in the rags
of a tormented and neglected
poor person,
in hopes that the encounter
will provide a place
for healing and hurt to meet,
for grace to embrace sin,
for beauty to be restored.

In My Nothingness

Only through humble eyes
can God be seen.
I am nothing;
God is everything.
But in my nothingness,
God gives me everything.
Humility helps
shatter illusions.
Humility is the truest form
of honesty.
It sees our weaknesses
and vulnerabilities.
Humility allows God
to transform our weaknesses
into strengths.

Humility is a pathway
to prayer.
Prayer is the doorway
to the heart,
the center of our being,
the place where we can
let go, let go of
pretense, pride, ego,
and a host of things

blocking us from
the true source of life,
the true source of love,
God.
In the innermost
chamber of the heart
we see the dissonance
between the Spirit of God
and our spirit;
it is here we struggle
to dissolve that disharmony.
In the safety
of the heart
we can let go of fear
and we can
risk change.
In the heart,
conflict gives way
to harmony.
In the heart,
what's mine
becomes God's.
In the heart,
humility becomes
holiness.

Grace and Resilience

Every day the news
presents to us
a world of
uncertainty and chaos.
In ourselves
we often see,
if we truly look,
a disconnect between
our faith and
our values.
Getting through
most days requires
a heavy dose of
grace and resilience.

We walk on a
very narrow path,
the cutting edge,
between
chaos and grace
as we struggle
to find
peace and purpose
in the present moment.
Short periods
of reflective
stillness and silence
help ease
the struggle.

Avatars for Change

*"Against this cosmic background the lifespan of a particular
plant or animal appears, not as drama complete in itself, but
only as a brief interlude in a panorama of endless change."*

—Rachel Carson, From in her poetic, 1937 essay "Undersea"

I have a friend
who said
with a determined,
strong voice,
"This is who
I am
and I will not
change."
I was too stunned
to offer any response
but silence.
Later, I felt only
sadness for her.
Does she not know
all of life is
continuously changing,
always evolving into
something new?

To resist change
is like being in
a coma.
You are there,
but not there;
you are in
a lifeless state.

From the moment
of conception we are
continuously changing
slowly over nine months
to becoming a human being.
From the moment
of birth
to the moment
of death,
we are
continuously changing.

But changing is not easy,
so, we resist it,
even fear it.
Change is often
forced upon us
by earthquakes,
hurricanes,
tornadoes,
a cancer diagnosis,
being fired,
a serious car accident
that leaves you paralyzed,
the death of
a spouse,
a son or daughter,

a mother or father.

Suffering changes us,
forces us to face ourselves,
makes us see what is
really important.
Love changes us,
makes everything
look more beautiful.

Without an openness
to change,
we will not
see or hear
the angel of grace
knocking on
the door of
our hearts,
our souls.

Every moment of the day,
from doing the dishes
to earning a living,
and every encounter
with another,
even a stranger,
is a portal to change
if we are open and receptive.

I was changed
by an encounter
with a homeless man
in Rome.
He was from Russia
and had served
in the Russian navy.

I gave him
something to eat.
He gave me
new insights
into poverty,
into the Gospels.

To live is
to change,
to evolve into
becoming fully
human.
Only God is changeless,
always loving,
always merciful.

St. Francis of Assisi
changed from being
a playboy and a soldier
into a humble man
who cared for the poor,
the downtrodden,
the neglected,
the excluded,
the sick,
the outcasts,
and all of creation.
He changed from
a sinner to a saint.
His transformation
was so complete,
even birds spoke to him
and a wolf listened to him.
The sun became his brother,
the moon his sister.
The new, transfigured Francis

embraced Muslims
and even lepers.

Francis became
a channel for
God's grace
to flow into others
in his lifetime
as well as
countless people
down through
the centuries.
All those changed people
touched and changed
untold numbers
of other people.
The ripple effect
is still touching
new shores.

A modern-day
spiritual son of the saint,
Maximillian Kolbe,
changed from
deriding Judaism
to giving his life
to save the life
of one Jew
inside a Nazi
concentration camp.

For me,
one silent moment
in an empty Franciscan church
in Rome
radically changed

the direction of my life.
I went from denying
the existence of God
to wanting to more
fully know
and experience God
in the depths of my being.

To not change
is to die.
We must continually
be transformed into
more loving,
more merciful,
more compassionate,
more forgiving
human beings
who radiate
the loving presence
of God.

I think it is helpful
to change religions
at least once in your lifetime,
to see things from
a different angle,
a different perspective.
The mystics of all faiths
all share the same message
of love.
My Muslim and Jewish friends
have taught me much,
have made me
a better Christian.

Doubt is a good thing,

as it is a path to change,
a path to God.
Discarding calcified dogmas
or dusty rituals
opens the door
to evolutionary
growth and change.

Things today are changing
for the worst.
These are divisive, angry times.
Many people fear
and even hate
those who are
different from them,
those whose race or religion
are different from theirs.
Instead of evolving,
people and nations
around the world
are regressing into
the darkness of hate
and isolationism.

All communal change begins
with changing ourselves.
As the caterpillar
morphs into a butterfly,
we too must change
from crawling along
the dirty ground of
selfish individualism
into flying to
the beauty of love
for all people
and all of creation.

Our home,
planet earth
is very sick
and without global
change will die . . .
probably not in
our lifetimes,
but we are headed
for a dead end.

Change must become
the new normal.
Evolution, emergence
is where we must live.
St. Francis was
an avatar for change.
We too need to become
prophets and avatars
for a change
that leads to us
becoming fully human
always loving into
a family of inclusion,
where no one is left out
or seen as disposable.

To forgive another
changes them
and us.
Every act of kindness
changes us,
brings us a step closer
to awesome, life-changing,
life-giving reality of God.
To embrace the leper,

the undocumented migrant,
the victim of violence,
or the stranger
brings a touch of heaven

down to earth and
changes heartache and harshness
into flowering beauty.

Thanksgiving Day
November 28, 2024

This "poem" came to me during my pre-dawn, sixty-five-minute walk on Thanksgiving Day. I cut the walk a little short so I could quickly get home and sit before my computer and start channeling the poem. It just flowed from me and was written in one take. I shared it with a few friends, saying it had nothing and everything to do with Thanksgiving Day. A little later in the morning, after some unexpected positive reaction to it, I added two short stanzas and a better ending. I must say I was inspired by the soulful and mystical poetry of Lucille Clifton and Pádraig Ó Tuama.

Also, after reading this reflection, a friend reminded me that Marcus Aurelius, the Roman emperor and Stoic philosopher, said, "Change is the only constant in life." We start this process with diapers. The Harvard psychologist Daniel Gilbert aptly observed, "Human beings are works in progress that mistakenly think they're finished." And then there is Rilke's "Sonnets to Orpheus": "Anticipate change as though you had left it behind you."

The life of faith is a journey, a perpetual pilgrimage searching for growth, for becoming ever new, for being renewed and converted. Nonetheless, as my late Irish friend Fr. Daniel O'Leary, who was an author and a columnist for The Tablet, wrote: "It takes a great love, and many deaths, to transform the eyes of our souls so as to see God's face in every face. And inevitably, inexorably, this love, this hope, will lead to a crucifixion."

Live Love

Contemplation and poverty
are natural partners.
Contemplation helps us to see,
to see both inside us
and to see around us.
Our contemplative vision
    improves
as our lives become
more simplified.
Our lives are cluttered
with so much stuff,
and we are so easily distracted
by so many things,
that our spiritual vision
is severely diminished.

We live in thick fog
of materialism and escapism.
Poverty of spirit
and simplicity
helps us see
what is important,
helps us see
another's need,
helps us see
injustice and suffering,
helps us see
the need to be free
from all attachments
that limit our freedom
and ability to love.

Contemplation leads
to communion.
The world is divided
into two camps:
the rich and the poor.
Between those two camps
there is no communication,
no shared life, no communion.
The rich and the poor
are strangers,
and their mutual isolation
gives birth to
misunderstanding and mistrust.
And the gap between
the rich and the poor
grows wider and deeper
by the hour.

Jesus condemned
the unnatural and unjust
division
between the rich and the poor,
because the division causes
pride, envy, jealousy,
self-centeredness and loneliness.
The Kingdom of God,
Jesus tells us,
is about unity,
reconciliation, harmony,
peace and love.
The Kingdom of God
is about oneness.

Jesus calls us
to a life of communion,
communion with God
and communion with each other.
The life of communion
helps us grow
in knowledge and love
of God and each other.

Jesus is the bridge
between the rich and the poor,
the bridge between
earth and heaven.
The cross of Christ
reconciles us to God
and each other,
and is a lived example
of self-emptying love.

Contemplation and communion
leads to action,
calls us to the margins of society,
to the American urban jungles
of deprivation, crime, and
     violence,
to the dark corners around the
     world,

where people live in massive slums
of overwhelming need
clinging to life
without clean water or electricity
and barely enough food for
     survival.
In these deprived places,
we not only give life,
but life is also given to us.
It is here
we see for the first time
the oneness
that has always been there,
though obscured by
our blindness.

Through contemplation
we learn to see.
Through communion
we learn to share.
Through action
we learn to love.

Be still.
Know God.
Live love.

Seeing Beauty

Do we walk
with an open heart
that allows us
to see
—*to really see*—
the beauty
all around us . . .
and within everyone?
The divine is
manifested
everywhere
and in
everything.

In Florida
seeing the sun
rise over ocean
or a homeless woman
sleeping on the
hard, cold ground
covered with
worn-out blankets
connect me
with the conflicts
within me.

In the bleak
ugliness
of the slums of
Haiti
it is difficult
yet essential

that I can see
the beauty of life—
the tenderness
of a mother's touch,
a hand reaching out
to help another—
even in a place of
senseless barbarity
that creates fear
and the darkness
of hopelessness.

The rising of the sun
helps me see
the inner beauty and
the connectedness
of all life.
I also can see myself
in the homeless woman
sleeping on the street.
I, too, am in a deeper sense
homeless.

I need to
carve out
space for the
stillness and silence
needed to open
my heart and eyes
to the replenishing
beauty of nature and art,
to wash away

the ugliness manifested
by hardened, unloving hearts
hungry for
meaning and power
and unconcerned for
the suffering of others.

For me,
to gaze on an icon
of Christ
helps me let go
of my inner
loneliness
and wounded spirit
and see the beauty
and the profound
communion of all life . . .
even in the barren, bleak
landscape of Port-au-Prince,

where you will see
what you should never see . . .
I cannot unsee
the horrific things
I've seen in Haiti.
A man set on fire.
Legs being amputated.
A person dying on the street
from a gunshot wound.
But I can disarm their impact
though the true beauty
of acts of compassion.

As Dorothy Day said,
beauty will save us.
Not superficial beauty,
but the true, deep beauty
of all life and
a surrendered, loving heart.

November 30, 2024

From Jonathan Montaldo:

"Through and out of your darkness a flare from the ship of your true mind and heart rises for us. You are signaling to us from the belly of life's deepest contradictions, another Jonas."

Thomas Merton: "I am thrown into contradiction. To realize it is mercy. To accept it is love. To help others do the same is compassion."

*Compassion is
far removed from
pity and sympathy.
Compassion grows
out of an awareness
of our common humanity.*

Half of humanity
must survive on
the equivalent of
two dollars a day, or less.
Half of that half
lives on less
than one dollar a day.

Jonah and the Whale

*In such a constricted and confounding place like Haiti, I was able to find comfort
and even enjoyment from the noble words of teachers like Raimundo Panikkar.
He showed me what the monastic impulse truly was:*

> *a tendency to move from dispersion to centeredness,*
> *from fragmentation to wholeness,*
> *from a "nothing but" attitude, boredom, and weariness*
> *to a meaningful life enriched by*
> *symbols, relationships, silence, prayer,*
> *simplicity of heart, enriched by*
> *the Logos of the soul.*

> I found in myself
> little interest in
> the distant goal of heaven.
> The hereafter was
> not what I was after.
> I wanted the
> fullness of Being
> now.
> This proved elusive.
> I was too fragmented,
> pulled in too many directions,
> yet feeling at home nowhere.
> I did not fit in . . . anywhere.
> Yet I made Haiti my home.
> Or, rather,
> I discovered my home,
> my purpose in Haiti.
> Maybe Jon Sobrino was right
> when he suggested
> there is no salvation
> outside of . . .
> *the poor.*

For me, Haiti was
my "Jonah in the
Belly of the Whale" experience,
my night sea journey.
Haiti showed me who I was . . .
and who I could be.
In Haiti, I began to move toward
simplicity and unification . . .
which are truly monastic goals.

In Haiti, I experienced
many deaths.
I am not talking about
deaths from violence
at the hands of barbaric gangs.
I mean "little deaths"
within myself.
Every day presented me
an opportunity to
let go of something
I had held too tightly.
I often resisted.
Blessed were the days
I did not resist.

Jonah was the Old Testament prophet whom God sent to a great and sinful city to deliver a message of forgiveness. Jonah attempted to avoid going at all costs because he was so irritated at the prospect of God's love for the immoral city and its people and His eagerness to forgive them. Since forever, humans have lived on streets of "us" and "them."

Hidden and Waiting

One morning in Assisi in 2008, a heavy fog concealed the sun and covered the town. It was mysteriously beautiful. It prompted me to jot down the following poetic meditation, which became part of the narration of my film The Loneliness and Longing of St. Francis:

A thick blanket of fog
is hiding the sun
and covering Assisi.

The innermost essence of God
is hidden from us,
totally separated
from the created world.
We can see only hints
of God's love,
which is enduring and
    incomprehensible.
God is utterly transcendent
and lovingly immanent.

The call to holiness is
an invitation
to enter fully into
a committed relationship
with God.
As we respond,
God graciously nurtures growth
in the relationship,
by using events, circumstances,
    and people
in our lives as instruments
to hasten a contemplative

outlook on life.
Prayer becomes
a vital part of our day,
and, in prayer,
we encounter more fully
the Author of our life.

This personal encounter
with the Creator
slowly transforms us
into a Divine likeness,
as it gently erases
all traces
of the un-God-like substance
within us.
In prayer, we unlock
the vault to
our deepest self
and allow light
to shine on God
who is already abiding
at the very core of our being,
a tangible Presence
hidden from us
yet patiently
waiting for us.

I confess God sometimes is still so hidden I doubt Her existence. But doubting God's existence is not a bad thing; in fact, it might even be beneficial to the life of faith. Fourteenth-century Dominican mystic Johannes Tauler believed that part of any growth in faith was the experience of being "abandoned [by God] in such a way that we no longer have any knowledge of God and we fall into such anguish so as not to know any more if we were ever on the right path, nor do we know if God does or does not exist."

Back in 2008 (and many times over the years since then), I was in such a place of anguish, doubt, and confusion. It is part of the life of faith, because faith is not a static or unchanging force; faith has ups and downs, peaks and valleys. Even Mother Teresa of Calcutta experienced long, tortured periods of great darkness, even years of it. In that darkness, she wrote in her private diary: "I am told God loves me—and yet the reality of darkness and coldness and emptiness is so great that nothing touches my soul."

There will be days when our faith lacks any sense of presence, that it is out to lunch or on a prolonged hiatus. But the very desire to feel or sense our faith points to the reality of our faith, that it exists and is real. If our faith is alive, it is always growing, changing, and maturing . . . or else it is slowly dying. Prayer is the oxygen of faith. Mother Teresa continued to pray through the darkness, and she continued to see the beauty within the lost and lowly sleeping in the gutters of Calcutta.

"God is a mystery nobody wants. What people covet in God is not mystery but certainty. God is what everyone seeks to be sure about. And is not."

—Joan Chittister, *In Search of Belief*

Far and Near

Speaking on behalf of the Lord,
the prophet Isaiah said,
"Hear, you who are far off,
what I have done;
you who are near,
acknowledge my might."

There is a loneliness
to the past and the future.
I am not there;
I am here in the present.
I am far from
who I was in the past
and far from
who I will be in the future.
I am only near myself
in this present moment.

God, too, is far and near.
Far in the sense
that God leaves us
to ourselves
in order for us
to discover our own hearts
and the heart of God.
Yet God is as near
as the next breath we take,
as near as our very heartbeat.

God is so near
we do not see Her.
God seems so far
because we do not know Him.

Because we do not see
or know God,
who is so far
and so near,
we have the anguish
of loneliness
at the core of our being.
We know emptiness,
not plentitude.
Sadness is always
around the corner;
joy occasionally comes
and quickly goes.

To discover God
in your heart
you must journey beyond
all self-consciousness
to an awareness
of a reality greater
than yourself.
It is a long journey
and a short journey.
On the journey
we must drop
all notions of God
and
all notions of self.
Only then can
God reveal God
to you
and reveal you
to yourself.

In loneliness and longing,
we begin our journey to God.
Stripped of everything,
we have nothing,
we take nothing.
Yet our very loneliness
is graced
with the possibility
to discover
the transcendent.
Even the silence of God
is graced and speaks
of the mystery of God
and God's forgiving nearness,
God's hidden intimacy.
In stillness and silence

we learn about
a love that shares itself,
an overflowing love
that dissolves all alienation
and fills the empty space within us.

God is here in this moment,
waiting with
open and outstretched arms,
waiting to embrace and caress you
with endless love.

Kiss this moment
for in it
is perfect joy
and all good.

House of Fear

Today in Haiti,
hope is in short supply,
cowering in a
house of fear,
fearing being shot
or kidnapped
or decapitated
or burned alive,
and worried about
running out of
food and water.

Every day for nearly
ten years in Haiti
I encountered people
who were
hungry and thirsty
not only for
food and water
but for justice and

relief from the
perpetual hopelessness
and mindless violence,
which has only grown
worse and more intense
in the last two years.

Five million Haitians
are facing
acute hunger.

There is no
common table of
love and fraternity
in Haiti.

In Haiti and many other places
around the world,
we have become separated
from the original oneness.

The Heart of All Reality

I was in Haiti during Advent of 2009. Three weeks after my departure, on January 12, 2010, a devastating earthquake rocked Haiti, killing over 3,000 people and leaving a million people homeless. I returned to Haiti days after the earthquake on a private jet with a team of twenty-six doctors and nurses. I was in Haiti for Lent and Advent in 2010. In the summer of 2010, I lived in a slum in Port-au-Prince for two weeks. The following reflection comes from my film Mud Pies & Kites, *which was filmed during all those visits to Haiti.*

Across America the year ends
in a flurry of shopping,
even during stressful economic
    times.
Advent helps us see the need
to pause and contemplate
the deep and magnificent meaning
of the Incarnation:
that God, in a supreme act of
self-emptying love,
became poor for us,
entering fully into
our flawed humanity
in order that
we could have the chance
to enter more fully into
God's perfect divinity.
Advent was the perfect time
to be in Haiti.

The primary motivation
for God's incarnation is
God's goodness,
not human sinfulness.

The Incarnation is
a dynamic expression
of God's overflowing
love and mercy,
as well as a revelation of God's
poverty and humility.
Through the Incarnation we find
redemption and completion,
making it the heart of all reality.
Christmas is a time
for us to see more clearly
our own poverty and weakness
to better receive the gift of
God's transforming love.

In Haiti, it was easy to see how
Christmas is a time for us to
    emulate,
as best we can,
God's love and goodness
by sharing the
mercy and compassion
we have experienced
through our lived experience

of Christ's birth
in the stable of our humble hearts.

In the slums of Haiti,
I am stripped bare
of all pretentions,
all sense of superiority.
I stand in the midst
of the swirling, turbulent world
of overwhelming want,
feeling the pain
and not knowing how to respond.
But God says
let my eyes, my hands, my mouth
become your eyes, your hands,
    your mouth.
With my mouth, give a smile
to each sad face.
To the person who has become
hardened and hopeless,
give them my heart.

This is the gift of Christmas:
the heart of God
born afresh within each of us.

As "The Song of Zechariah" says:
"In the tender compassion of our
    God
the dawn from on high shall break
    upon us,
to shine on those who dwell in
    darkness
and the shadow of death,
and to guide our feet into the way
    of peace."

In Advent, we live in
the expectancy of
a changed world,
a world of universal sufficiency
and no hunger,
a world of peace and nonviolence,
a world where
the reign of God
is fully manifested.

But such a changed world
is still a long, long way off,
a seemingly impossible dream,
especially here in Port-au-Prince.

The chronically poor living in
the slums and tent cities
are constantly on the move
but never going anywhere.
Just up and down
back and forth
the same roads
every day
in search of
whatever is needed
just to survive.

They walk, they haul,
they jam into tap-taps.
Constant movement,
incessant noise.
Every day is a wearisome,
endless struggle,
without a hint of comfort
or relaxation.
Congested streets.

Maddening traffic.
Dense pollution.
Smoldering heaps of garbage.
The tension is unrelenting.

Every day is a fresh, new
challenge . . . to do
the same thing:
find whatever
is needed to survive that day.
The effort that goes into
just making a few pennies
to buy the barest of essentials
is extreme.
Every day is exhausting.
And the night offers
no relief.
The misery just
gets darker.

Pain still abounds
nearly a year after the earthquake.

Violence lurks
around every corner.
Grisly crime and corruption
are commonplace.
Rubble from toppled buildings
is everywhere.
Backbreaking labor
paying only pennies.
Hunger and illness
inhabit most
homes, shacks, and tents.

Yet there is tenderness,
smiles, and faith . . .
and even hope in the face of
utter hopelessness.
The people keep going,
keep struggling
to inch ahead,
to care for their families . . .
and prepare to celebrate
the birth of Christ.

Sadly, after the assassination of the president of Haiti in July 2021, many gangs came together to fill the political void in the wake of the killing. By the summer of 2024, the gangs controlled 85 percent of Port-au-Prince in a yearlong tsunami of barbaric violence that included beheading and burning people alive.

In Advent 2024, the gangs killed more than 150 elderly people in one night in the largest slum in Haiti. In 2024, the gangs killed an estimated 5,600 people and forced over 700,000 people to flee their homes with only what they could carry. In the first six months of 2025, nearly 3,000 additional people were killed, including a wonderful female doctor who operated on one of my kids. She was shot in the head.

People lived in fear
and without hardly
a flickering of hope.
Into this turmoil,
Jesus was born.

In February 2025, a gang member took a three-month-old infant from her mother, who was breastfeeding her baby. The gang member then threw the baby into a fire the gangs had started. Within hours the mother died from the horror of what she had witnessed. The barbarity of the gangs knows no limits.

The Heartbeat of God

Our hearts are broken,
wounded by a thousand
little cuts and bruises.
Jesus came
to heal our hearts.
Through his sacred heart
the heart of God is revealed.

To contemplate and imitate
the Sacred Heart of Jesus
is to contemplate and imitate
the love of God.
Through Jesus's heart
God loves us
and shows us
how to relate
to the Divine
and to all of humanity.

Jesus is the heartbeat
of God.

The heart is
the center,
the core
of our
bodies,
spirits,
and souls.
The heart is the home
of our deepest thoughts,
our deepest desires,
our deepest longings.
It is in

and through
our hearts
that we come
to understand ourselves
and learn how to
relate to others.
The heart is
fundamental to
physical and spiritual life.

In the physical heart
of Jesus,
the spiritual heart
of God
was incarnated
and made flesh.
Jesus loves
with a human heart,
a human heart
that beats with
Divine love.
Our human hearts
need to be
transformed into
sacred hearts,
Divine hearts
that beat with
human love.

We were created
for relationship.
Love is the doorway
to authentic, life-giving
relationships.

The Heartbeat of the Incarnation

The following was part of my narration for me film Where Love Is, *which featured the Capuchin Soup Kitchen in Detroit, Michigan.*

Christ gave us an understanding
of Divine justice
that is based on
Divine mercy.
The heartbeat of the Incarnation
is generosity and love.
In Christ, we see a God
    so generous
He throws everything away
    out of love.
Christ moved beyond justice
    to generosity.
Jesus took pity
    on the crowd's real need
and called on his disciples
    to feed them.
Jesus prayed for
    daily bread.
Jesus defended those who,
    in their hunger,
ate the grain growing in
    someone else's field.

While we busy ourselves
striving for power
and trying to control
events and even people,
the Gospel perpetually proclaims
a far different approach to life:

God has created us
to live a life of
dependence and receptivity,
and our acceptance of
that spiritual reality
is required for true human
growth and fulfillment.
To live the Gospel forces us
to live with contradiction—
for the Gospel requires a faith
which believes that
when one has nothing,
one has everything.
Moreover, it asks us
to count poverty as riches
and humiliation as an honor.

Service to the poor and lowly
is not optional . . .
it is an obligation
for the disciple of Christ.
To turn your back
    on the poor
is to turn your back
    on Jesus.
If the Gospel is not about
    love and justice,
it has been reduced to
    mere sentimentality.

Jesus denounced power,
injustice, and poverty.
The core of Christianity is about
the cross, suffering,
renunciation, and sharing
what we have with others.

The Capuchin Soup Kitchen
exemplifies
the very heartbeat of the
Incarnation.
They give away everything,
sharing *their* lives with others.

A Privileged Path

Jesus chose to be poor.
We wish he had not.
We are embarrassed
by his poverty.
His poverty makes us
uncomfortable.
Jesus suggests that poverty
is a privileged path,
that the poor possess
an eminent dignity.

We do not get it.
We do not choose
to be poor.
We run from poverty;
we hide from poverty.
Poverty makes us uneasy.

In America, demonizing anyone
who stands in the way
of your making a buck
is standard business practice.
For us, there is nothing "blessed"
about being poor.
But the truth is: I am poor.
I am in constant need.
I am impoverished
by my many weaknesses,
my many bad habits.

I am at the age
when each day

I am impoverished
by the lack of time
I have left to do the things
I want to do.

To understand poverty,
one must enter
the poverty of another,
as Jesus entered
our poverty.
The poverty of a
homeless woman
named Loretta in Skid Row,
the poverty of a drug addict
named Michael in Kensington,
is my poverty.

Our poverty is blessed
when we do not possess
anyone
and we are free
to be possessed by
everyone.
In my poverty,
I can possess Jesus . . .
and give Jesus away.

Watch how a person treats
the poor and the hungry,
the sick and the stranger,
and you will know
that person's view of life.

Putting God in a Box

Out of the traces of God
we happen to detect,
we create concepts of God
and ideas about God
that have little or nothing
to do with God
because we simply do not
know God.

Until God intervenes,
all we can do is
stumble along
in the direction of God.
But God is far-off,
and so, we make do,
coping as best we can,
struggling as we walk.

We think we are in control.
And so, we feel
a measure of peace.
However, to find God,
we must lose control,
drop our need for security—
and this is the last thing
we want to do,
so we really don't look . . .
we just pretend we are looking.
We put God in a box
and are happy . . .
which is, ironically,
the source of our unhappiness.

Turbocharged

Most Americans live
turbocharged lives,
addictively driven
to pursue status
and possessions.
Our compulsive drive
for more is
making us sick.
Our frenzied lives
distract us from
what is truly important:
relationships with
other people.

In the world of business,
greed has reached
epidemic proportions,
which is choking to death
the chances of true happiness.
We seek and want more
than we need.
We are so busy
getting more
we can't enjoy
what we have.
It is no wonder
depression is
on the rise.
We must slow down
and curb our appetite,
and find creative ways
to create meaningful work
and a more equitable
distribution of wealth.

Facing My Aloneness

On the morning of December 3, 2024, not long after 4:00 a.m., I cracked open *Nothing Personal,* James Baldwin's blistering essay on social isolation and race and began reading part three of the book. I was only a few paragraphs into it when I realized I was a long way from being a good writer. I lacked the imaginative skills to look deeply into common items easily overlooked as we go about our busy days, such as a cracked vase, or the mundane experiences, such as facing a new day, when the bitter reality of yesterday is still lingering in our mind or pressing on our heart. Baldwin skillfully addresses the competing need to be alone and the need to be with another. We need space to be with ourselves, and we need the tender touch of another.

In my forced exile into aloneness, I am seeing more deeply into myself. I am happy to have the space and time to focus on my new book, which has been a heavy cross to carry because I didn't have either the time or space needed to finish it. So, now I sit alone staring at the text, making little changes, cutting some text, and adding new text. But my mind wanders and is easily distracted. News, mostly bad, from Haiti discourages me. Donations from supporters encourage me. The daily ups and downs of the day take a toll on me. I am tired of all the administrative work required to keep Santa Chiara open during these stressful, violent days in Haiti. I long to travel . . . to Rome or Dublin or Istanbul . . . but I don't want to leave my comfortable apartment in Vero Beach. I light up when I see the smiling, exuberant face of Clare Marie on a video call from Haiti. Yet the sad stories of all the kids who have lived with me at Santa Chiara weigh me down.

The new book (*The Cross of Love, The Pain of Poverty*), which few will read because it is too long, too scattered, has forced me to relive many of the poverty films I made . . . all of which have searing images of poverty-induced suffering around the world. Here in upscale Vero Beach, Cho the homeless man I pass either on foot or in my car disturbs me . . . as the does the predawn sight of a homeless woman sleeping on the street with the temperature in the mid-forties. Will the new day bring him or her any hope, any relief? I just recalled a homeless man I interviewed in the dead of winter in Philadelphia. I trained the camera on his face as I asked him one last question: "Do you ever experience any joy?" A quizzical look crossed his face, as he slightly turned his face to the left and skyward as if he was looking for an answer. Finally, he looked directly into the camera and softy said, "Joy?" . . . as if he did not even know what joy was. It seems stupid to say to Cho the homeless man, "Have a good day."

I miss Haiti. That is a lie. I am embarrassed (or ashamed) to admit I do not miss Haiti, that I do not want to go back to Haiti. Ever. But I know that I will, as soon as commercial jets are allowed to fly to Haiti or the airlines determine that Haiti is safe enough for them to land in gang-infested Port-au-Prince without their planes being shot at. In Haiti, I would miss the days of silent listening much more than air conditioning and hot water. The sounds of silence are symphonic. In Haiti, the only beauty I ever see is the smile of a child or the sight of someone helping someone in need. Compassion is always beautiful. Forgiveness is oxygen. In love, there is no betrayal.

We have drifted far from
the Divine ideals of
love and compassion.
All around the world
we see the extremes
of cruelty humans can reach
and the pain we can inflict
on each other.
We have become trapped,
imprisoned by our own egos.
We have forgotten
our capacity for love,
our need to love our neighbors,
which includes strangers
in faraway places
who look different from us.

In the stillness and silence
of my aloneness,
many of my wounds
from a long life
arise from a deep sleep
to hurt me again.
A knife in the back.
Another failed relationship.
Dreams dashed.
Plans gone awry.
In time, the wounds and failures
recede to wherever they live.
Long walks help.
As does listening to
instrumental music,
mostly classical,

with a splash of jazz . . .
and Gregorian chant
in the early morning
always goes well with
Haitian coffee.

Sadly, we are living in
a loveless, lonely world,
in a time when
all human connections are
    distrusted.
Today I want to feel
the connectedness of all life . . .
and to be at home with myself.
Maybe one day that will
    happen . . .

if I really want it
and remove all the obstacles
to making it happen.
Meanwhile, today I will enter the
    pages of
*The Cross of Love, The Pain of
    Poverty*
and try to be a better writer.
I will light a candle to James
    Baldwin
and Abraham Joshua Heschel
and Vincent van Gogh
and Thomas Merton
and John O'Donohue.

s
i
l
e
n
c
e

s
i
l
e
n
z
i
o

Darkness Is Enough

*"Your brightness is my darkness. I know nothing of You
and, by myself, I cannot even imagine how to go about
knowing You. If I imagine You, I am mistaken. If I
understand You, I am deluded. If I am conscious and
certain I know You, I am crazy. Darkness is enough."*

—Thomas Merton

*I had to type those true and powerful words from Merton to feel them in my
fingertips. We talk too much about God and thereby reveal our ignorance. The
darkness of unknowing engulfs and discomforts me.*

I felt a speck of Light
in an empty church
in Rome in March of 1995.
Since then, I have lived
in total darkness,
walking in the shadow
of the poor.
I had no idea
where I was going.
I just went where
the wind of the Spirit
blew me.

I saw the face of God
in the faces of
the ignored poor
enduring endless degradation,
insufficiency, and suffering.

I tried to be a light for them,
to tell them they were not alone,
not completely abandoned.

I sometimes walked through
massive slums by myself,
with only my camera,
unable to speak
in a foreign tongue
yet somehow connecting
with people simply through
my presence among them.
In Skid Row (Los Angeles),
I was at home
with the homeless.
It was magical.
It was mystical.
It was a miracle.

"One discovers the light in darkness, that is what darkness is for; but everything in our lives depends on how we bear the light. It is necessary, while in darkness, to know that there is a light somewhere, to know that in oneself, waiting to be found, there is a light. What the light reveals is danger, and what it demands is faith."

—James Baldwin

A Monet Painting

In 2004, I was invited to speak and show part of my film Endless Exodus, *which documented the plight of undocumented migrants entering the United States, at a luncheon of the Inter-Religious Council of Southern California. The gathering of Buddhist, Islamic, Hindu, Jewish, and Christian leaders was held at the Board of Rabbis office in downtown Los Angeles. I ended my improvised talk with the following scripted remarks penned for the occasion:*

I want to leave you with this thought:
Think about a painting by Monet.
If you were to get very close to it,
all you would see is
random daubs of paint,
imperfect-looking individual brushstrokes.
Yet when you step back from the canvas,
you see fields of beautiful flowers.

Each of us here,
representing different faiths,
different denominations,
are like those imperfect brushstrokes
of a Monet painting.

The essence of a Monet painting
is its organization,
the combination of hundreds of
individual strokes of paint
working in harmony
to create something beautiful.
And that is what we are called to do:
to work in harmony to bring
hope and healing to those who are suffering
from the cruel effects of chronic, unjust poverty.

At the foundation of all our different faiths
is compassion.
We show our love for God
by how we treat
the least of God's children,
no matter their faith.

And this involves more
than giving our spare change.
We need to go out and embrace
the anawim in our midst,
embrace the poorest of the poor,
those completely overwhelmed by want,
without voice or rights
in their surrounding community.

The Jewish Scripture
makes it abundantly clear
that to forget the anawim
is to forget God.
Jesus made care for the anawim
a litmus test for our love of God.

As Elie Wiesel said:
"When someone suffers,
and it is not you,
they come first.
Their suffering gives them priority.
To watch over another who grieves
is more urgent than to think about God."

May God bless you
and give you peace.

The Day of Atonement

From sunset on Rosh Hashanah, the Jewish New Year, until sunset the following day, Jews around the world engage in solemn introspection amid a joyful celebration and continue to reflect that week until the intense repentance on Yom Kippur, the Day of Atonement, at sunset. It marks the end of a period of repentance that began on Rosh Hashanah. On Yom Kippur, Jews reflect on their sins or wrongdoings from the previous year, ask for forgiveness, and think about how to improve for the coming year. Our secular society has lost the notion of sin and repentance.

While making my film *Endless Exodus*, I came to see our treatment of undocumented migrants as sinful, and so I choose to end the film with a prayer Jews say on the Day of Atonement. Here is the concluding narration of the film:

> Almost a year ago, in August of 2003,
> as I drove across the Arizona desert
> heading for Mexico,
> I was ignorant about the plight of the migrants.
> Before crossing the border,
> I had no idea where the journey would take me.
>
> This film taught me one essential lesson:
> We must not judge others.
> It is so easy to condemn
> the migrant sneaking across the border,
> but we must resist the temptation
> to judge them or hold ourselves up
> as better than them.
>
> We are all brothers and sisters.
> We are all connected.
> The ideal of compassion
> is based on a keen awareness
> of the interdependence of all living things.

We live in a world that is filled with pain.
The planet is covered with people
who are overwhelmed by suffering.
Wars, famines, economic injustice, diseases,
and natural disasters are killing people every day.
I've seen a little of it.
We are impotent when it comes
to making the pain go away.

Life is hard and messy and painful.
Hurt abounds and hope is in short supply.
Jesus did not clean up every mess
or relieve all the pain he encountered.
Jesus simply told us to take the pain
and the mess of our lives
and place them before God.

Even then, the answers to the riddles of our lives
are not always perceivable or even obtainable.
Jesus teaches us to live with the questions,
to live with the pain.
Peace, he suggests, is found in faith.

God is bigger than we are,
and we, in our weakness,
need to lean on the strong arm of God.
Cures and answers may not come to light,
but faith, hope, and love changes
who we are and how we deal with
the messiness and pain of life.

Our spiritual life will not prosper
without an intense awareness
of our own poverty and emptiness.
The source of wisdom
is hidden in the shadows of life.

This film has been about journeys,
the physical journey of the migrant,
as well as our and their spiritual journeys.
In his last book, *The Asian Journal*,
Thomas Merton reminds us,
"Our real journey in life is interior;
it is a matter of growth, deepening, and
an ever-greater surrender
to the creative action of love and grace."

I would like to end with a prayer
Jewish people pray
during the Day of Atonement,
the holiest day of the Jewish year
marked by a twenty-five-hour fast
during which all work and business
are forbidden except God's business:

> *"For the injustices we condoned*
> *and the times we kept silent*
> *and our unwillingness to learn*
> *and our self-pride,*
> *O God forgive us,*
> *pardon us,*
> *and grant us Atonement."*

Grace Is Everywhere

In *The Diary of a Country Priest,*
French novelist Georges Bernanos
has his dying curé exclaim,
"Grace is everywhere."

Every once in a great while,
I'm able to see things
as they truly are,
able to see that grace
indeed seems to be
everywhere.
The beauty of catching
a glimpse of abounding grace
is that it makes
my own limitations
feel less severe
and makes God's vastness
appear even greater
than I ever imagined.

The painter Paul Gauguin
    claimed
he shut his eyes
in order to see.
The Sufi mystic Rumi advised
selling your cleverness
and buying bewilderment.
What they are saying is
that the heart sees
what the eyes can't.
St. Francis learned that lesson
    very well
and was willing to let God
flip his world upside-down.

Conversion is listening to
the events of your life
that change your perspective.
Francis understood he had a need
for an ongoing change of heart
and ongoing change of perspective
that allowed him to see
the way God saw
and allowed him to see
grace everywhere.

It was his willingness
to be "grasped" by God
that made him unique.
He approached each day
with a simple,
very childlike attitude:
God, what do you have in store
for me today?!
This outlook released him
from the burden of
self-groundedness and
into the freedom of being
grounded in God,
thus allowing himself to
    experience
a realignment of his passion,
and a complete recentering
of his affections.

For Francis, conversion was
a liberating experience,
freeing him from
the prison of self rule.

Seeing God's Grace

In October 2006, I gave a ninety-minute "Poverty and Prayer" presentation at a daylong religious education congress sponsored by the Santa Barbara pastoral region of the Archdiocese of Los Angeles. I was asked to show my thirty-two-minute film When Did I See You Hungry? *During the ninety-mile drive along the coast from Los Angeles, I could not help but be overwhelmed by the natural beauty I observed. I began my talk by speaking about the beauty I saw on the drive up the coast to Santa Barbara.*

It's easy to see God's grace
in the natural beauty of creation.
Far harder is seeing God's grace
in the horrific slums around the
world
where I have spent a great deal
of time
over the past five years.

But that is our challenge:
to see God in the ugly places
we would rather not see at all.

Earlier this year, I spent two
weeks
living in a home in Lima, Peru,
that housed fifty destitute and
sick kids.
The kids had every disease
imaginable.

There were blind kids,
kids with missing or deformed
limbs,
kids with leukemia and cerebral
palsy.
There were severely malnourished
kids,
and kids with cleft palates.

It was a place of
great suffering and sadness,
and a place of
great hope and joy . . .
thanks to
a heroic and prayerful
American doctor.
While living there
I learned a lot
about poverty and prayer,
and a lot about the beautiful
mystery
of life and death.

Between Night and Day

As each new day dawns,
God's light gives us
a renewed pledge
of God's love,
a fresh beginning
that is a pure gift,
a gift meant to be given away
during the day.

In the silence between night and day,
I feel God's grace and peace
and am commissioned
to become an instrument
of that very same grace and peace.
In the splendor of new light,
God's love and mercy are revealed.

*O God help me to see
the radiance of Your light
and show me this day
how to be a servant of Your peace.
Help me, O God, to share
the delicate, intoxicating fragrance
of Your mercy and love
with those whose lives
are lived on the shadowy
and dismal margins,
with those whose days
see no happiness,
with those whose days
end without hope.*

The Difficult Journey

Everyone experiences heartbreak;
everyone is in need
of tenderness and compassion.
At some point in our lives,
we all have to face
the difficult journey
of coming to terms with feelings
of rejection and humiliation and fear.
These very real and very painful feelings,
in time and in prayer,
become an authentic path
from despair to hope.

Tragedies and disasters become
places of courage, of perseverance,
places where we learn to plumb
the depths of our inner life,
our true essence,
and are able, by God's grace,
to move from rejection and terror
to healing and hope.
Love grows from
that deep-rooted pain
within the universe
where God is present
and ever-willing to
embrace us and bless us.

Where Love Is

When we are enslaved
by obsessive desires
we are not free to pray.

When our interest in
power, money, and material things
is greater than
our longing for God,
we are still far from
authentic prayer.

The deeper we journey
into prayer,
the less interested we are
in thoughts rooted in
worldly desires and sensory
    perceptions.

Our prayer should be dressed
in reverence and humility,
unsoiled by a mind
still cluttered, impassioned, and
    impure.

Calm the restlessness of your
    mind with mindfulness of
    your breathing
and by acts of compassion and
    mercy.

The altar of our spirit
should be unadorned
and free of
false and unhealthy desires.

We must imitate God
who stoops down in mercy
to touch us.
So we too must
stoop down in mercy
to touch others . . .
even those who live far away.

The spiritual life
is a twofold journey . . .
an inward movement
to the depths of our being
and the source of Love
and an outward movement
to the broken world,
the margins of society,
where love is manifested
in acts of kindness.

Meek and Humble

Humility is
the cornerstone of
repentance.
Sadly, humility's stock
has declined in our time.
Instead, we value
a sense of pride,
a sense of self-glorification,
a sense of self-righteousness.
Today, many people view humility
as a sign of weakness.
How easily we forget
the words of Christ:
"Learn from me for I am
meek and humble in heart."

Repentance, deeply rooted
in humility,
is a return to
the right order of things.

Repentance is the path
out of exile.

Repentance is more than
"pleading guilty"
to transgressions.
Repentance needs to acknowledge
our alienation from God,
our failure to enter fully into
the joy of communion
with the Divine.

Repentance is not merely
a response
to a spiritual indictment;
it must also be
a response
to the fact that we have
strayed from
the glory of God.

Either/Or

Contemplation and solitude
increase our ability
to become
more compassionate.

Compassion frees us
from the "either/or" dualism
that chokes us
and leads us
to a reconciliation of opposites.

As we grow in compassion,
we see more clearly
how the world is
interconnected.

Compassion opens the door
to heaven.

What happens
to a poor person
living in the slums
of Nairobi, Kenya,
is happening to you.
We are one.
Compulsion, competition,
and dualism
deny that unity.

The Way of the Cross

Christ's suffering and death
on the cross
led to
his resurrection.

When we become one
with Jesus, forsaken
in the suffering of others,
we both experience
ourselves passing through
the cross with Christ
into the resurrection life
of Trinitarian love and unity.

When we embark
on the way of the cross,
we travel through suffering
and discover the Love
that is God
within us.

The Sacred Heart

The sweet, gentle,
merciful, always-loving
Heart of Jesus
beckons us to join
our heart with His,
to fully join in
His incarnation,
passion, death,
and resurrection
on a daily basis,
opening our hearts
to deeper levels
of love, humility,
evangelical poverty,
compassion, and
unselfish service to others
so that we may one day enter
into full unity with God.

O Most Sacred Heart of Jesus,
so often broken by my sinfulness,
have mercy on me
and draw me closer to You today.

A Question

The radical message
for which Christ died
is dramatically opposed
to our culture
of egoistic individualism
and unchecked consumerism.
Should not our Christian faith
compel us,
by means of our transformed hearts,
to live differently
from the rest of our culture,
whose values are rooted
in the material realm
and are far from
the teachings of Christ?

The Sweetest Word

Much of life hurts.
Forgiveness helps
life hurt less.

Sadly, our hurts
often become
who we are,
forming our very
identity.

Forgiveness helps us
forget our ego,
our pain,
our feelings.

Forgiveness is possible
when your heart
overflows
with compassion.

Forgiveness is
freedom,
radical freedom,
Divine freedom.

Outside of forgiveness
God is unknown
and unknowable.

Forgiveness is
the sweetest word
there is.

Weakness

The more you pray,
the more you will become
poor, plain, and empty—
and ready for God.

Prayer consists of becoming
aware.

We experience God's love
in proportion to our experience
of our own weakness.

Day in and day out,
God the Divine sower
liberally plants seeds
in the soil of our lives.
Prayer tills the soil,
making it receptive
to the flowering power
of the seed.

But far too often
the soil is hardened
by sin, worries, and
an unhealthy preoccupation
with money, power, and success,
and so the seed
is trampled on
or blown away.

We talk a lot about love,
but the concrete experience of love
is a rare thing indeed.
We claim God's love
created the earth
and that same love
appeared on earth
in Christ.
But we do not see it
or feel it.
God's love goes
unnoticed.

To make visible
the hidden love
of God,
to feel more intensely
the inexpressible marvel
of God,
we need to spend time
in prayer
and time with
the poor.

Because each of us is
a child of God,
each of us possesses the eminent
    dignity
of a child of God.

Divine mercy is incarnated
in human weakness.

Communion

If the Gospel has become
flesh within you
then every person
is your sibling.

The best way to love God
is to relieve the pain
and suffering of others.

Our concern for the poor
is both political and mystical,
and bringing the two strands
of human experience together
is our great challenge in the face
of the tsunami of soulless capitalism
and class warfare
that are washing over
so much of society.

We seek to make
connections.
God calls us into
communion.

Our lack of reverence
is destroying earth
and crippling relationships.

Empty Hands

Punctuate your day
with thoughts of God,
recalling God's unselfish,
self-giving love for us.

Do not be seduced by
perishable things.
Detachment reflects
the realization that
God alone matters.
The world demands
more and more from us.
God only asks for
empty hands.

At its essence, prayer is
not about asking for Divine favors.
The primary purpose of prayer is
to assist us in continual
abandonment to God.

Prayer essentially is loving God,
which is why we need
to deepen our prayer life
to deepen our love.

Prayer consists of
becoming aware.
Prayer is the
breath of life.

God Is

God is . . .
no need for
more words.
God is . . .
enough.
Muslims have
ninety-nine names
for Allah,
each expressing
an aspect of God.

God is . . .
pure goodness.
God's goodness
shines through
all of creation.
The brilliant goodness
sometimes shines
brightly as in
a sunrise,
an epiphany,
a piece of music,
a painting,
an act of kindness.
At times,
God's goodness
is veiled,
hidden from our view.

The brightness
lets us know
God is . . .
present,
somewhere
beyond us,
somewhere
within us.
When the brightness
is hidden,
it is so
we look harder
to see the goodness
in others,
in creation,
and we too
begin to yield
to the goodness
and are
transformed
by the goodness.

God's goodness
is rooted in
a love
that is
the beginning
and
the end
of everything.
God's unending
and expanding love
desires that we live
in that Divine love
and share it

with others   compassion,
through acts of   mercy,
kindness,   and forgiveness.

The Tenderness of God

To live in the reality of God
is to live in trust,
transparency, and compassion.
To live in the reality of God
is to be embraced by
God's tenderness.

To be a follower of Christ
is to celebrate the
tenderness of God.

The same tender mercy
that sustains me
sustains my enemy.

We often find it very difficult
to offer forgiveness.
Not so God; for God,
forgiveness is effortless.
In fact, God takes joy
in forgiveness because
it generates new life.

Present Moment

"I Am,"
says God.
God did not say,
"I Was,"
or
"I Will Be."
In saying,
"I Am,"
God is saying,
"I am present."

Am I present?
Or do I live
in the past,
replaying old scenes,
clinging to old wounds?

Am I present?
or do I live
in the future,
chained to useless fantasies
and baseless fears?

God is beyond time
and always present.
But we look away.
We look back
and are hurt.
We look ahead
and are terrorized.

In this present moment,
God is facing us.
In this present moment,
we will no longer be
victims of the past
or be
paralyzed by the future.

In this present moment
we can face God.
In this present moment
we can encounter God.
Oh God, help me be
in this present moment.
Oh God, help me see
in this present moment
You.
Oh God, help me
see You
in all I do,
in all my encounters,
in all the people I meet,
in all of creation.

Dream & Write

This is a note I sent via email on March 22, 2025, to a young Haitian woman grappling with fear and depression induced by the endless, barbaric gang violence in Port-au-Prince. She dreams of being a writer.

Yes, life in Haiti is grim, fear is
   in the air.
Will I catch a bullet in the
   head today?
Will the gangs kidnap me?
People are trapped in their
   homes . . .
mostly shacks.
No running water.
Not enough to eat.
No dependable electricity.

It's no wonder
Haitians struggle
with despair.

Yet, we can still
dream.

Dreams, though fragile
and not deemed urgent,
are essential to
transforming lives
and corrupt systems.

Remember,
we have a collective right
to dream of a humane world.
Collective liberation
begins in the corners
of the human heart.

Write from your
lovely heart . . .
and breathe
deeply.
In stillness and silence
the Spirit will
speak, softly . . .
almost a whisper.
You will feel it
even if you can't
hear it.

In This Darkness

We are lost.
All is hopeless.
Look around, the evidence is clear.
War, hatred, violence,
lying, cheating, stealing,
and corruption abound.
Greed and lust
have all but become virtues.
There can be no doubt:
We are lost, all is hopeless.
We are powerless
to change anything.

But in this darkness,
God sheds a light.
What was impossible for us to see—
love, mercy, compassion, kindness, hope—
is possible with God.
God has the infinite power
to change everything.
But we have the on/off switch
to that unlimited power.
That on/off switch is
surrender and obedience.
To have access to God's power,
we must first surrender our own will
and then submit to the will of God.
The switch is right before our eyes,
but we choose not to see it.
We mask our blindness
and hopelessness with
an array of illusions and deceptions.

And so, the darkness remains
because without God
we are lost and all is hopeless.

"What do I want?"
is the question
we strive to answer.
Jesus would have us ask
a different question:
"What can I give?"

A Tender Lover

When Jesus encountered
the weak and hurting,
his very demeanor reflected
his gentleness,
his lack of aggression.

He was never imposing or pushy.
There was no judging or condemning;
he washed feet and liberated.
Jesus was a tender lover,
a healer whose encouraging touch
strengthened the feeble.

In his encounters
with the sinner and the rejected,
Jesus was humble and embracing.
His gentleness, compassion, and simplicity
are manifestations of his
great interior poverty.

Our mean-spirited
politics of food
reflects our great
spiritual poverty.
We want to push
the homeless
far away from our sight
instead of relieving
their miserable plight.

Making All Things New

The interior life is
the beginning of
eternal life.
Heaven does not begin
after we die.
It starts here and now
as we respond to
God's grace
by making all things new
and creating paradise
on earth.

Today, sadly, many people
seem to have forgotten
or have dismissed heaven,
thereby ignoring the idea of
eternally living with God.

We are so preoccupied
with the surface of life,
we do not pay attention
to the Divine call
to enter more deeply
into the silent streams of
a God-energized
life of the Spirit,
which transforms us
into more loving and
compassionate beings
who see beauty in everything,
who love the truth,
who thirst for justice,
and who embrace and protect
all of creation.

We watch TV,
we shop,
we fight,
we ignore the common good,
we applaud the rich and the
    powerful,
we snub the poor and the weak,
and we rape the environment.

The Desert Within

In 2021, I found the following in an unpublished book I wrote in 2007. I "knew" a lot of stuff about the spiritual life. The problem was that I didn't manifest that stuff more fully in my life. I still don't. The inner struggle is more exhausting and more troubling than the external struggle of life in Haiti. As I read it for the first time in over a dozen years, I felt I was attending a retreat given by me. My own words entered me and moved me . . . and, by God's grace, change me.

According to the Gospel of Mark,
the Spirit drove Jesus
into the wilderness.
Is the Spirit driving me
into the desert?
Seems like lots of things
are driving me,
but I rarely feel
the Spirit driving me.

Lent is a time the Church sets
    aside
for making space
for the Spirit,
a time to move away from
the normal distractions of life
and be renewed by
the Spirit of Life.
Lent is a time to look at
what drives me,
what excites me
and see if those things
drive me away
from the reality of God.

Lent is about empty spaces,
desert places,
that gives me the opportunity
to feel the Spirit drive me
into the desert of my heart and
    mind
to purge them
of all those desires
that are not healthy.
We don't have to wait for Lent
because we can enter
the spirit of Lent anytime.

In the wilderness for forty days,
Jesus was tempted by Satan.
The desert, with its lack of clutter
    and people,
has endless stretches of time
to look closely at
the wasteland of my life.
The desert challenges me
to come back to my true self,
the self that was created
in the image of God,

an image I have tarnished
by my self-destructive behavior,
my yielding to the drives and
    desires
that do not reveal the beauty
    of God.

The desert reveals
my essential neediness
and vulnerability.

But the desert,
with its vast horizon
of empty space,
is a place where I learn
that I am not alone.
In the desert, you find the
        Spirit
who shows you how to be
your true self.

I shared this in prose form in my Haiti Journal on March 9, 2021. A very close friend, Jonathan Montaldo, who knows me better than anyone else said this to me in an email: "Your life is the book you have been writing over and over to find THE clue that will allow you to understand the puzzle and finally see a pattern you can be satisfied with, that you can 'live' with."

Four years later, the "pattern" is slowly coming into focus during my forced exile in the desert.

**Come, Holy Spirit, fill my heart and
kindle in me the fire of your love.**

The Edge of Humanity

Beginning in the Old Testament
and boldly traveling down
through the centuries
to our own time,
the prophets have all spoken
loudly and clearly
about the absolute need
to care for the poor.
Yet we mostly have ignored
those living hidden lives
on the margins of society,
living, suffering, and dying
in dire need.

The great Jewish rabbi
Abraham Joshua Heschel,
whose writing on the prophets
is the quintessential text
for understanding
the role of a prophet,
said a prophet
"employs notes one octave
too high for our ears."

All the prophets spoke out
against the exploitation
of the poor and the weak,
people living on the edge of humanity.
A religious faith that does not fight
against all forms of injustice,
including racial and economic injustices,
was intolerable for the prophets.

As people of faith,
we are compelled by God
to see injustice and
to work to eradicate it.
In the eyes of God,
this is,
according to the prophets,
more important than ritual worship.

Living on the Edge of Extinction

There is a darkness
that is enveloping
the world.
We live in
soul-crushing times.

Before the cease fire agreement in late January 2025, the people of Gaza lived lives of extreme oppression and poverty. Gaza was (and remains) a giant open-air prison. Two weeks into 2025, the Palestinian death toll from the war was 46,560; many feel the death toll is underreported and is much higher—perhaps 40 percent higher. In one week in the new year, seventy Palestinian children were killed. It is incompressible. (The ceasefire ended, and the killing resumed, as the surviving people in bombed-out Gaza starved to death.)

The suffering and death in Haiti are off the charts. The death toll from the unremitting gang violence in 2024 is estimated to be over 5,600. As of October 2024, over 700,000 Haitians, including children, were forced to flee their homes due to gang violence. Hospitals have been vandalized and destroyed. Doctors have been kidnaped and killed. Haiti is a cesspool of violence, vice, dishonesty, and corruption. Killing is a sport for the blood-thirsty gangs that control Port-au-Prince; the politicians who control the levers of power are gangsters in suits. The suffering of the poor is of no interest to the gangs or the politicians. Life is cheap. Death is meaningless. Kids are expendable. Hunger is widespread.

The helpless people in Gaza and Haiti are human beings whose dignity has been stripped from them, whose lives do not matter, whose suffering does not merit our concern. When it comes to their suffering, we are indifferent. I feel compelled to write about the insanity, to point out, over and over, how this violence defies the tenets of all religious faiths.

Why would anyone read what I write? They have lives, things they must do, things they want to do, things they love doing. Why would they spend any of their precious time reading about the horror in Haiti or the terror of poverty here in America and around the world. Outside of a few friends and family, no one has any interest in my spiritual journey and evolution.

As a filmmaker I have witnessed far too much suffering caused by poverty, war, and inadequate medical care for the poor. Suffering is a huge part of life. I have a friend in California who is nearing death. A friend in Northern Ireland took a dreadful fall that will take many months to recover from. A friend in New Jersey is fighting deep depression. A friend in Iowa has been living in an assisted living facility for many months, hoping one day he will walk again. I cannot forget the woman surgeon in Haiti who operated on my Haitian daughter and two weeks later took a bullet to the head from the hand of a gang member. I still mourn the death of Tamysha. The question at the top of the previous paragraph is pointless. I do not write to attract readers or sell books. I write to heal myself. I write to communicate the importance of compassion, mercy, and kindness.

Still, how do I get anyone to think my writing is worth their time? Certainly not by improving my weak writing skills; there are talented writers who write about nothing. When I pick up my pen (or create a blank page on my computer), I must bleed on the page, sacrifice myself. I must be vividly real, unashamedly honest, and truly concerned about the suffering of the marginalized, the rejected, the ignored, and the victims of racism. I need to write to heal myself of the sickness of our collective life as it has evolved (or devolved) during my lifetime. Meanness and divisiveness have become normalized. Ours is a fragmenting, anxious world.

If I were looking to attract readers, I would not be writing about all the things that trouble me . . . like the genocidal destruction of Gaza, relentless bombing of Palestinians, the desperate, near hopeless plight of everyday Haitians, the lives of malnourished kids in Uganda, the disfigured lepers in Brazil (as well as in Jamaica and India), the victims of drug-related violence in Honduras, a dying kid with incurable skin disease in El Salvador, handicapped kids in Peru, undocumented migrants living in the shadows of cities in America, people living in a refugee camp in a desert in Kenya, the people in the Philippines who survive by rummaging through mountains of garbage, naked kids sleeping on the streets in Calcutta, people who die in the desert in northern Mexico trying to find a new life in America, the homeless man in America who is afraid a rat will enter his mouth as he sleeps in an abandoned building in the dead of the winter in Philadelphia.

> I entered the bloated belly
> of poverty . . . and I can think of
> nothing else.
> The triviality of life
> in America
> saddens me.
>
> I write to share
> what I have witnessed
> in the poorest places on earth,
> places where people live
> on the edge of extinction,
> just hoping to survive the day.
> I write to share
> the importance of imitating
> in our own way
> the ideals of Christ
> who made care for the poor
> a litmus test for eternal life.

The Dwelling Places of the Lepers

St. Francis of Assisi encountered God
in the dwelling places of the lepers.
The lepers helped the saint
understand and heal himself.

Today, we encounter lepers
on a daily basis—
they are the homeless
sleeping on park benches
or in crime-ridden shelters;
they are the deinstitutionalized mental patients
begging on our corners;
they are the jobless
offering to wash our car windows;
they are the poor children
dying from preventable diseases;
they are the refugees
flooding across borders
with nothing but the clothes on their backs
and hope in their hearts;
they are the drug addicts and alcoholics
sleeping in subways and vacant buildings;
they are the truly destitute eating in soup kitchens
where day-old bread and donuts are served;
they are the AIDS victims
dying alone in hospices.

Today's lepers are
the two-thirds of humanity
who live in crippling poverty.
Enter their dwelling places
and share their misery,
and encounter
the love and mercy of God.

A Field of Poppies

Our spirits need
time to rest,
to wander in
a field of poppies,
to soar with the sunrise,
to swing in a hammock.

Our spirits need time
to simply do nothing,
which, oddly enough,
will give us the ability
to do everything better.

Solitude gives us insight
into our deepest needs
and feelings.

Tranquility of heart and mind
springs naturally from
the well of solitude.

God speaks
in silence.

Fragments

Sin is all the stuff
that sends us down
a dead-end street.

The path to God
runs through
your daily life.

What we profess
to believe
must be actualized
in our daily life.

Different religions
are like branches
but God is the root.

All of Creation

From the March 17, 2016, Haiti Journal

"Christian life is a commitment to love, to give birth to God in one's own life and to become midwives of divinity in this evolving cosmos. We are to be wholemakers of love in a world of change."

—Ilia Delio

All of creation flows from
a good and loving God;
therefore, all of creation
is good.
All of creation is
an expression of God's love.
Because God is
the author of all life,
we, along with all of creation,
are brothers and sisters
who are called by God
to be one in cosmic harmony.

All of humanity is
connected to God and
created to live in relationships.
All humans were created to
    emulate
the self-emptying love of God
and to share God's love
and mercy with each other,
especially with those
living on the periphery of society
and imprisoned by chronic
    poverty.

Note: I spent a few days traveling in Italy with Sr. Ilia back in 1999. She is a Franciscan nun and an acclaimed scholar.

Good Friday

In 2011, I spent Good Friday in Cité Soleil with Fr. Tom Hagan. I filmed him as he conducted a brief prayer service. The gangs had threatened to kill some of us if we processed through the slum. The threat was so real, I called a friend in Los Angeles who had recorded all my narration for all my films to tell him thank you for all his help . . . as I was not sure I would survive the day. My friend was not available to answer the call. I left him a message which he never erased.

Despite the threat, after the prayer service, Fr. Tom, with the help of a few seminarians, hoisted the large wooden figure of Christ on his shoulders and began a long march through Cité Soleil, followed by a procession through the slum of people singing and praying. It was a truly inspiring walk past the endless shacks that lined the main street. It was at least a twenty-minute walk from the school to the wharf, where we turned around and walked back. I was grateful the threat did not materialize.

The God whom Jesus reveals
is not a God consumed with
   power,
but a God interested in
   relationships
of caring fidelity,
a God who is in solidarity with
the most vulnerable and most
   needy.

Jesus gives and forgives.
When we walk with Jesus,
God's generosity is guaranteed,
making greed and the frenetic
   pursuit of
acquiring more and more of
   everything
both inappropriate and
   unnecessary.

Jesus gives us new marching
   orders:
Love one another.
In the eyes of Jesus,
a brother and a sister
is everyone,
even those who
don't look like us,
don't act like us,
don't believe like us . . .
and even those
who make us uncomfortable
or hate us.

Jesus calls us to an
alternative way of life,
a way that says no
to control, power, and
    domination,
a way that says yes
to trusting in the abundance of
    God.
Our culture and our government
do not embrace such a way of life.

A fundamental principal
of the Gospel insists
that the weakest and least
    presentable people
are indispensable to the church.
Sadly, the church, just like the rest
    of society,
seems more enamored
with the wealthy and powerful.

The central message of Jesus
was this:
God must be understood,

not as power,
but as compassion.

We have no fervor
for the Cross.
We have other interests
and do all we can
to avoid the Cross.

Saints seem to have a devotion
to the Cross.
One saint said,
"God is in the Cross,
and as long as we do not love the
    Cross,
we will not see him or feel him . . ."

Such fervor for the Cross seems
    extreme.
Yet somehow, I fear it is true.
I know I want to avoid the Cross.
I know my heart is full of things
    not of God.

And so, I pray:

O sweet Lord,
I want so very much
to avoid the bitter cross
You ask me to carry,
the cross of putting aside everything
that is outside the realm of Your love.

Actually, nothing is outside
the realm of Your love,
because You so long for us,
so thirst for us,
that You follow us
into the darkest corners of our lives
looking to embrace us
with Your mercy and compassion.
Yet I so often want to embrace things
that You find unhealthy and unfitting
for a seeker of God.

O Lord, help me see, feel, and know
that outside of You
there is nothing of any worth
and that with You all is priceless.
Help me nail to the cross
the secret things in my heart
that I must sacrifice
in order to follow You
more closely and love You more dearly.

A Short Distance

Following Christ
is not easy
or for the
faint of heart.

I often find myself
caught between
devotion and doubt,
fidelity and failure.
I can praise Christ
and hours later
betray Him.

It is a short distance
between the praise
of Palm Sunday
and the torment
of Good Friday.

Holy Week invites us
to follow Christ on the
Way of the Cross
by renewing our efforts
to stay faithful to Him
to the very end.

Not easy.
Even Jesus did not carry
the cross alone . . .
Simon helped him.

We too must also help
others—the outcast,
the homeless, the migrant,
even the criminal—
carry their crosses.

As we extend
a hand of help,
it will cost us.
Our lives will be
disrupted,
we will become
bone tired,
we will be
betrayed and mocked.
We might even need
to exhaust our
financial resources.

It will hurt
to help
the hurting . . .
and we do it anyway.
Our focus becomes
others.
Our nourishment comes
from prayer.
Grace becomes
our lifeline.

Love and Goodness

Things in Haiti today seem hopeless, as the gangs take more and more control over all facets of life . . . and death. The past should teach us that the sense of total hopelessness does not last. The following is from an Easter Sunday scene in my film Mud Pies & Kites, which was produced in the aftermath of the horrific earthquake on January 12, 2010. Easter is closer than we think. Resurrection happens every day.

In the face of such massive
destruction
and monstrous loss of life in
Haiti,
it is easy to lose faith,
to begin to doubt
and even succumb to
hopelessness.
The misery was inescapable
and indescribable.

Haitians and well-intentioned
outsiders
are quick to offer an array of
social, economic, and political
solutions
to the problem of widespread
suffering,
but nothing changes
and the misery goes on
virtually unabated.

The only way that Haiti will
recover, rebuild, and renew itself
is with love and goodness . . .

and huge amounts of both
for a long period of time.

It really is time we rebuild our
lives,
our communities, and our world
on the eternal principals
that cannot be destroyed by
brutal dictators, gangs,
terrorists, or earthquakes.

We need to see God
in each other.
We need to turn away from
hatred
and more fully embrace
love.
We need to make compassion
the foundation of our lives and
actions.
Tolstoy said that our great duty
as humans
was to sow the seed
of compassion
in each other's heart.

It is only compassion
that will change and save the
    world.
Anne Frank reminds us,
"How wonderful it is
that nobody need wait
a single moment
before starting
to improve the world."

Easter beckons us
to build bridges to unity,
bridges to a distant shore
where common ground is found
and peace prevails.
Easter is a time of healing,
a time for us to embody
Christ's work of reconciliation.

Our very woundedness
is waiting to be transformed
into compassion.
Our emotional and physical pain
helps us understand and respond
    to
the suffering of another.
Compassion is as elegant
as any cathedral.

At Easter, we proclaim in song
    that
"Christ is risen."

And He truly has.
Yet, when we look at the reality
of the world around us,
we see death and destruction,
revenge and retaliation.
Our culture of death
dominates
our spirit of life.
We have lost
our prophetic voice,
and we no longer defend
the stranger, the widow,
and the orphan,
those who are hurting
and have no voice.

Cité Soleil and places like it exist
because we as the human family
have forgotten God
and turned our backs
on God's children.

We need to share our time,
our treasure, our love
with the chronically poor.
Jesus wants us
to give our lives away.
This is Gospel giving.

In giving of ourselves,
Christ is truly risen.

Clinging to Earth

From the February 22, 2016, Haiti Journal.

The Cross is a symbol of tension,
a place where the vertical (heaven)
and the horizontal (earth) intersect.
The Cross is also a sign of sacrifice,
a place where Christ
listened to God,
trusted God,
was obedient to God,
and became one with God
in an act of total abandonment.

For us the tension between
the vertical and the horizontal,
between heaven and earth,
comes with our failure
to radically trust God.
Unlike Jesus, we hold back,
hold on to the things of the world
while God is continually inviting us
to conform our lives to
Christ's self-emptying love.

We strive for heaven
while clinging to earth,
and so are caught between
heaven and earth.
Jesus is the bridge
between earth and heaven . . .
and the bridge is the cross.

Pilgrimage

I cannot learn about God.
I can only unlearn the things
that are keeping me from
a full awareness of God.

To find Christ you must
make a pilgrimage to
the center of your being,
to the place where
the human and the Divine meet.

The key to being a pilgrim
is to remain still interiorly
as you journey . . .
otherwise, you are just a wanderer.

To pray is to embark
on a journey without end—
a journey deep into
the heart of darkness,
of paradox, of mystery.

The journey to God is slow.
Each day, we inch our way
along a steep, winding road.
The pace of spiritual
    transformation
moves about as quickly as
traffic in Los Angeles.

Spirituality is essentially a journey
in which we move
from what we are
to what we will be;
it is a journey to weakness.
We truly learn to live
when we begin to explore
our weaknesses.
Every experience of weakness
is an opportunity of
growth and renewed life.
Weaknesses transformed by
the reality of Christ
become life-giving virtues.

A Journey to God

It's good to realize
we are on a journey,
a journey to God.
What are we taking with us?
Me . . . I'm lugging a lot of stuff,
far more than can fit
in a knapsack.
Mostly, I'm carrying my sins.
They wear me down,
slow me down.

Slowly as I travel, I'm learning
to see that my sins
do not erase from my soul
the fundamental dignity
that God stamped on it
at my conception.
God does not want
to see my demise.
God's mercy continuously desires
to give me new life.
Sin alienates me from God.
But God does not reject me
because of my sin.
God simply wants me
to refrain from sinning,
because my sins prevent me

from experiencing the love
God wants to shower upon me.

For so long, I thought my sins
were beyond redemption.
They had me bound so tightly,
it was impossible to free myself
from their choking control.
But I didn't understand
the power of grace.
I underestimated the unlimited
power of God.

Dimly, I'm beginning to see
that God can overcome
my personal weakness.
All I must do is let Her/Him.
But before God can work,
I must wake up
and admit I need
God's help.
Genuine, sincere contrition
is always fully embraced
by God's tender loving mercy.

Lord Jesus Christ,
have mercy on me, a sinner.

Mystical Eyes

Each day brings
its share
of sweetness
and bitterness,
of joy
and misery,
of comfort
and pain,
of laughter
and tears,
of hopes
and disappointments.

Each day brings
rejection and acceptance,
loneliness and communion.
Each day brings moments
of fear and despair
and courage and delight.
Each day brings
a flood of words
and a desert of silence.

Each day we have
moments of
transparency and deception,
moments of
faithfulness and infidelity,
moments of
strength and weakness,

moments of
purity and lust,
moments of
beauty and cruelty,
moments of
abundance and famine,
moments of
peace and turmoil.

And each day
God is present
in all these things,
in all the ups and downs,
in the heartache and elation,
in the victories and the defeats.

But God's presence is
hidden and silent.
It is only through faith
we can see and hear God,
even though our seeing and
     hearing
are gravely impaired
and far from perfect.
We really don't know God,
yet we do know God.
In our not knowing
is the beginning of our knowing.
But the fullness of knowing
will always be beyond us,
yet hidden within us.

To see God
in all things
each day
is the mysticism
of everyday life,
the ordinary mysticism
that sees the extraordinary
work of God
even in the mundane events
of everyday life.

With everyday mystical eyes
we are able to see God
in both the cries of the poor
and the laughter of a child,
in both a tender kiss
and in a deadly disease.

Sister Orange

Some days I take
delight
in the simple
peeling of
an orange.

On those days,

I feel
the presence
of God,
and I am
thankful for
Sister Orange.

A Silent Symphony

Before bed at night
surrender the anxieties
of the day
into the tender hands
of God's love.
Rest in peace;
arise in hope.

To bring to a new day
yesterday's pain and failures

is the easiest way
to darken the new day.

Every sunrise
is accompanied by
a silent symphony
of hope and peace,
which can only be heard
by a surrendered heart.

Symphony of Life

Love is
the symphony of life.
It needs to be
practiced and played
every day.

God is
the composer,
Christ is
the conductor,
and we are
the performers.

New Neighbors

People have been
and always will be
moving
from place
to place,
either on their
own initiative
or forced to migrate
because of
war, famine,
economic opportunities,
or fracturing societies.

I have lived in
six different states
and in seventeen different
locations within those states.
I was only comfortable
in one of those places,
Carmel-by-the Sea,
California.
I have even lived
in three different locations
in Port-au-Prince.
Now I am
most comfortable
living among
the poor.

A sense of belonging
is not about
being tied to

the place of your birth
or any single location.
The earth itself
is always changing,
always evolving.
Vast changes in
the life of a
city or country
continuously push
people to live
in new places.
Migration has always been
part of the human story.

Sadly, we do not always
welcome the stranger,
the migrant fleeing
war, poverty, hunger, or
climate change,
such as severe drought,
and environmental disasters,
such as earthquakes.
We do not always welcome
people whose race or religion
or culture or language
is vastly different
from ours.

The migrant and the refugee
have become unwelcomed,
isolated,
and shunned outcasts.

In the eyes and heart
of Jesus,
they are merely
new neighbors
for us to love and help.

Human migration has become
heavily politicized.
Politicians often disparage
     migrants
by dehumanizing them

and creating fear of them,
which causes racism
and social injustice.
Like earth itself,
migrants are used
and abused.

We are changing
our environment
as we are being changed
by it.

Two Things

Christianity lives in the heart,
not the head.
The head is for doctrine.

Live for God.
Literally, explicitly,
without shame.

Finding our way back to God
requires only two things:
faithful love and sure trust.

In the state of emptiness,
you are better able to encounter
the fullness of God.

In our helplessness,
God can do
anything.

Daunting Yet Essential Questions

Who am I?
I mean deep down inside,
at the very core of my being . . .
Who am I?

Is my true identity,
my true self,
something created in
the mind of God,
or is my identity
something shaped by
the external forces of
my birth, my family, my friends,
and the very circumstances of
    my life,
such as where I live and work,
and maybe even by what I eat?

Is my identity formed
by chance or choice . . .
or by the hand of God?
Did God have a purpose for me?
If so, is my identity inexorably
    linked
to that Divine purpose?

These are daunting
yet essential questions.
Answers seem speculative
and suspect at best.
My experience tells me
God is real.
Furthermore,
my experience reveals
that God is love.

If God is love,
and I therefore
came from love,
it seems logical that
my true identity
will only be revealed
in the perfection of love
within me.
Most days,
that does not seem
to be happening.

The Wings of Love

Love is
the most uplifting force
in the universe.

Love gives birth
to miracles.

Real love is
never tempered with
prudence nor
controlled by common sense—
no matter how admirable
those qualities are.

Love is service.
It is the emptying of self.
It is losing in order to find.

We can only love truly
when our hearts are free
of the self-centered desires
of pride, ambition, and lust.

Charity is
love's visible form.
Acts of charity are
the wings of love.

Undressing

Strip away
all that is
inessential
and you will
find, in time,
the true
God
and your true
self.

Stripping away
the superfluous
is how you get
to be
the person
you were created
to be.

You can travel
much further
along the path
of authentic spirituality
by carrying less
while mixing
solitude with
kinship with
other seekers.

African wisdom
claims that if
you want to travel
quickly
go alone.
If you want to travel
far
go with others.

Ignorance and Arrogance

The mind needs
no training in how
to destroy through
willful memory loss
whatever in its past
doesn't support
its present point of view.

Whatever you believe
to be true today,
you should be willing
to accept
as false tomorrow.

It is necessary for
one experience
to die
so another experience
can be born.
Life is a series of deaths,
the disappearance of
values and ideas

that no longer serve.
Something I thought
was true yesterday
died overnight.
Today I am
mourning.
We are striving for
stability
in a world that is
unstable
and constantly evolving.

Despite all my study,
all my work,
I still live in
the shadows of ignorance.
In my arrogance,
I think I know everything.
When it comes to God,
very few know
very much.

No Blueprint

To live is to struggle,
day in and day out,
with all the
foibles and failures
that are part of
being human.

The path that does not
challenge
is going in the
wrong direction.

As we walk down
the path of life
confrontations with
the inexplicable
lurk around many
a corner.

The future has
no blueprint.
Anything
can happen.
Everything
that matters
is a mystery.

On the Flip-Side

It would be nice
to meet someone
who had faith
without having
answers.

Is it possible
to learn enough
to erase doubt?

The more informed
I become,
the more confused
I become.

If only for a day
I could take refuge
in the comfort
of certainty.

But on the flip-side,
certitude is
followed by
repose.

Made for Love

We talk a lot
about love, but
the concrete experience
of love is
a rare thing indeed.
We claim God's love
created the earth
and that same love
appeared on earth in Christ.
But we do not see it
or feel it.
God's love goes unnoticed.

We were made
for love.
But we are too busy
for love.
The lack of love
is giving birth
to depression and violence.

Love is
a hunger for
community.
Love exaggerates
the good in people.
Grace is
the breath of love.

Let yourself be loved;
let yourself be
acted upon by God.

The universality of
God's love
excludes no one.

Only an open
and serene heart
can absorb
God's love.

Acts of love
give flesh to
faith and hope.

Love Is the Key

Jesus asks us to love
as God loves—
without counting the cost
or holding anything back.
Love gives all away.
Love frees us to act
for the good of another
rather than for ourselves.
God's love is
unbiased and all-embracing.
It does not ask
who we are
or how successful
we are at what we do.

Being an instrument of peace
requires us to embrace
the enemy in pardon.

To give freely
what we have freely received—
namely, God's love—
is the purest form
of evangelization.
Following the example of Christ
will lead us
to go poor among the poor,
without power,
without purse,
without provisions,
with charity and respect
for those we encounter.
We must seek peace
above all else
and then do good
at every opportunity.

If our efforts at sharing God's
    love
are warmly received, fine;
if not, we should move on.
Our lives are our sermons,
and our preaching should be
benign and gentle,
spoken with
meekness and humility.

Diversity

The universe is clothed
in diversity,
yet humankind seeks
and religion claims
one truth.

Diversity is not
the cause of disunity.
A garden consists
of many plants
but is still one garden.

We are called
to realize the unity
of creation.

Solitude allows the soul
to look upon
the pieces and
see the unity.

Beyond Knowing

To be intensely religious
means not subscribing
to any religion.
If you are a member
of any church
you are required
to attest to their
morality and legality,

which are far from
the intrinsic nature
of the religion.

God is too big,
too beyond knowing,
to be fully contained
in any religion.

A Lonely Man

In isolation
a lonely man
searched for
the deeper meaning
of life,
of his life.

He longed for
connection
to another,
to a true faith,
to a community
were he felt
he belonged.
He found
none,
and his loneliness
and longing
intensified.

He was always
reaching out
to others,
aways searching
for resolutions
to the paradoxes
of life.

In every stranger
he met
he saw
a lifeline
lifting him from
his inner loneliness,
his feeling of
incompleteness.
None did.

The lonely man
is not alone.
We are all alone.
We all exist
in our own
isolation.
We are separate
beings
somehow connected
to everything.

In silence
we face ourselves,
our loneliness,
our connectedness.

Beyond Our Borders of Comfort

My faith is sprinkled
with doubts.
This has always troubled me
since coming back to the faith
in 1995.
I thought my faith
was supposed to be
strong,
yet I thought my doubts
had weakened my faith.
This was not only wrong,
but probably more common
than people of faith admit.

Recently, I began
thinking of my faith
more as
a *questioning* faith.
I see the questions
in a positive light
because they lead me
to a better understanding
of the heart of Christ
and His revolutionary insights
into the approachability
and experience of God.

By his life and teachings,
Jesus moved people toward
inclusivity, mercy, and justice.
He emphasized
loving your neighbor.
He preached nonviolence
toward all
and compassion for
the outcast,
the marginalized,
and the poor
living in squalor
on the peripheries of society.

Essentially, Christ calls us
to a peaceful fraternity
that extends beyond
our borders
of comfort.
Love needs to become
more and more
self-emptying
and more
giving.

Brothers & Sisters

We are all created by
the Creator,
and so we are all
in relationship with one another.
We are all brothers and sisters,
and to set yourself up as
higher or better than others
is a subtle form
of blasphemy.
We are all connected.
If one among us
is diminished,
we are
all diminished.

We are one
with all of creation
and the Creator.

We must seek harmony
in diversity
as we rejoice in
our humanness.

The Incarnation compels us
to step to the back of the bus
and sit with the poor,
to learn to see life
from their point of view
so as to better share
in their struggle for
access to God's gift of
freedom, oneness, and love
that has been denied to them
by virtue of our selfishness.

Digging Deeper

Our spirits need time
to marinate,
to soak in,
and absorb God's love.

What do we expose
our spirits to
through the daily choices
we make . . .
in what we read
or watch on Netflix?

Do our choices
draw us closer
to the light
and peace of Christ—
or to the darkness
of a world torn apart
by divisiveness,
racism, and violence?

In the woods of
in the Berkshires
of Monterey,
I more easily feel
the presence of Christ.

Long ago the Desert Fathers
were drawn to
the wilderness

to better experience
the silence and solitude
needed to be more fully
present and attentive to God.

"What is required," counsels
St. Theophan the Recluse
in the *Philokalia*,
"is a constant
aliveness to God—
an aliveness present when
you talk, read, watch or
examine something."

Walking in the woods
has rekindled
a spirit of hope
to better navigate
the present growing
chaos and madness of
Haiti, Gaza, Ukraine,
and America
with courage and faith.

We need to dig deep
within ourselves
to rediscover
the Divine presence
that calls us to an authentic
love, peace, and unity.

Commercials

The commercial advertisements
that fuel television
deliver one common message:
Do not be satisfied
with what you have—
only more "stuff"
can make you happy.

The life of Christ
makes it clear
that God chose
humility over majesty,
that infinity dwells
in the finite.

The common good,
which is the
breath of freedom
and the social bond
between people,
is being choked by
the iron fist of individualism.

Those living on
the margins of society,
the poor, broken,
and rejected,
are portals through which
we can enter fully
into the mystery of the Cross.

If you greet sunrise
with God in your heart
and a prayer on your lips,
your day stands a better chance
of reflecting God's love,
mercy, and justice,
and you will be better able
to treat others
the way God would.

Erased and Displaced

In Trump's America,
Haitians legally here
are being
erased and displaced
because they are
black
and powerless.
They obeyed
the law and
they are being handed
a death sentence.

They are being
sent home
by a racist president
even though
their home is
a war zone
of barbaric killings
by decapitation,
by being burned alive.

Nuns, priests, doctors,
and even children
are not spared
from death
by a bullet
made in America.

Blacks in America
know the pain
of racism.
They had to fight
for the most basic
civil rights
in a country
that prided itself
on the ideals
of democracy
yet allowed
rapes and lynchings
to go
unpunished.

People of Love

Let yourself be
loved;
let yourself be
acted upon by God.

To love others
as Jesus loves them
is an extremely difficult,
if not impossible, task,
yet it must be
our primary goal
as Christians.

God can't pour love
into a vessel
that is already full.

God loves me because
I am weak and powerless,
not in spite of those qualities.
I am poor and needy,
and God lifts me up.

There is nothing so
steady and relentless,
so committed and enduring,
so firm and unwavering
as God's love for us.
Over and over again,
in story after story,
Jesus tells us that
the defining characteristic
of God is
not anger
but love.

Yet we stumble around
in a fog of misplaced guilt
and wrong attachments.
As children of God,
we are called to be
people of love,
people who accept
God's love and
people who
transmit God's love.

Authentic Transformation

Outside the inevitable
suffering
caused by
death and accidents,
most suffering
bubbles up out of
our craving for
transitory things
and our worldly
attachments.

It is easy to become
attached
to the kind of
secure certainty
peddled by
religious fundamentalism.
But this kind of "knowing"
is a roadblock
to true knowing.
Clinging to the comfort
of certainty
is just as bad as
all our temporal attachments.

It is difficult for God's Word
to enter
our inner temple
because its entrance
is blocked
by our endless
array of attachments.
To be heard,
God requires
silence and detachment
from us.

Without daily
contemplative silence
it is impossible to have
a true encounter with
God's Word within us,
where authentic
transformation
begins.

A Hand of Mercy

My decades-long pilgrimage
in the footsteps of St. Francis,
taught me the importance
of fully embracing Christ
in the suffering of humanity.

Following Christ
means embracing mercy.
Christ sees our sins
and extends to us
a hand of mercy.
When we stumble
Christ helps us
to get up.

Jesus was drawn to
those living on
the peripheries of life.
Jesus mercifully engaged
those who were ostracized.
He did not judge
the outcast or sinner.
His offerings of mercy
opened hearts
to a new life of love.
Jesus did not focus
on a person's mistakes

or sinfulness.
Instead, he showed people
their intrinsic dignity
as children of God.
This was how love
is born and spread.

We are living in
a polluted environment of
mistrust, polarization,
scapegoating, and
the malignant impact
of social media,
which promotes
tribalism, recrimination,
cancel culture, enemy-making,
and a mistrust of science,
which taken together
stifle chances for
a more harmonious future.

In these turbulent
and troubling times,
Christ points the way
to nonviolent peace
and the way of love.

Addicted

We are victims of
overstimulation
and have become
addicted to
anything loud and fast.

Wholeness is attained
when we achieve freedom
from the greedy tendencies
of the ego
and its insatiable hunger
for possession.
A person becomes whole
when the self
learns how to be empty,
willing to lose itself
in order to enter into
a deep and rich
communion with others.

Through charity,
God lives in us
and we live in God.

Charity is
love animated.

The Grace of Forgiveness

Our main job in life
is reconciliation . . . with God,
with ourselves, with each other,
and with all of creation.
To be a follower of Christ
is to be open to
the grace of forgiveness.

Christ asks us to forgive
those who have offended us;
He goes so far as to say
we must love our enemies.
Reconciliation is the key
to personal liberation.

The Struggle for Liberation

In the Sermon on the Mount,
Christ said
the hungry will be satisfied.
It can happen—
but only when we
stand in solidarity
with the poor
and accompany them
on their journey.
As we walk together,
common concern
will overcome
the destructive tendencies
of individualism and greed.

The Gospel compels us
to unite with the poor
in their struggle
against poverty.

Service to the poor
is not optional—
it is a requirement
for the follower of Christ.

The poor see reality
with a clarity of vision
that is rarely reached
by the comfortable.
Walking among the impoverished
improves our vision.

We are able to see injustice
and feel pain.
We see how dehumanizing
dire poverty is,
and we want to join in their
struggle for liberation
from the chains that bind them.

Today's global economy
fosters soulless consumerism
and a mindless worship of
      technology,
while trampling
the rights of workers and the
      poor.

Exposure to those straddled with
dire poverty
uncovers our
clinging selfishness.

We have become so isolated from
the poor and the suffering
that we have lost the chance
to find true fulfillment
by giving of ourselves.

The Old and New Testament
say with one voice:
To walk with the poor
is to walk with God.

The Gospels make it
abundantly clear
that God is
on the side of the poor,
the broken in body and spirit,
and the outcasts of society,
the lepers, the prostitutes,
the orphans, the refugees,
and the addicted.

The true moral fiber of any society
or community or family
is revealed by how it treats
its weakest member.

Christ shows us that mercy
is more than

compassion or justice.
Mercy requires us
to become one with
the poor and hurting,
to live their misery
as though it were our own.
Jesus took his place
with the condemned,
an innocent deliberately allowing
himself to be arrested.
God's love gives everything,
always.

We can only truly love
when our hearts are
free of the self-centered desires
of pride, ambition, and lust.

Facing Myself

My exile from Haiti
is less a time
to heal myself
and more of a time
to know myself.

In exile
I am facing
myself
and hearing
the music
of eternity.

The past is
dead;
the future is
alive,
but short.

In Florida
I have
no social life
and do not
fit into
the local culture.
In Florida,
I essentially live an
isolated and lonely
life.

Haiti is my home.

Bumping into Things in the Darkness

Do the choices I make
reflect my deepest values?
When I look back
at my life,
I must not
romanticize or exaggerate
any of my past actions.
I must not see
idealism or nobility
where there was little
of either.
I was often
bumping into things
in the darkness.

I stumbled into
Haiti.
It was easy to condense
the reason for going there
as my wanting to stop
filming the poor
and instead go
live with the poor ...
implying that God
was directing me to do so.
If only such clarity
existed when
I stepped off the plane
in Haiti.

In retrospect, I see that in Haiti I was beginning to understand what being a follower of Jesus required from me.

A Follower of Jesus

To be a follower
of Jesus
is to prefer
life over death.

To be a follower
of Jesus
is to prefer
peace over war.

To be a follower
of Jesus
is to prefer
freedom over oppression.

To be a follower
of Jesus
is to prefer
forgiveness over revenge.

To be a follower
of Jesus
is to prefer
reconciliation over alienation.

To be a follower
of Jesus
is to prefer
contrition over excuses.

To be a follower
of Jesus
is to prefer
helping over hurting.

To be a follower
of Jesus
is to prefer
humility over pride.

To be a follower
of Jesus
is to prefer
vulnerability over power.

To be a follower
of Jesus
is to prefer
weakness over strength.

To be a follower
of Jesus
is to prefer
letting go over acquiring.

To be a follower
of Jesus
is to prefer
mysticism over materialism.

To be a follower
of Jesus
is to prefer
silence over noise.

To be a follower
of Jesus
is to prefer
prayer over idle chatter.

To be a follower
of Jesus
means I must be
willing to have
everything about
my life
be transformed.

PART TWO

Prayers

A Silent Symphony

Each morning,
we are awakened
to the presence of God.
When our hearts and minds
are awakened by God,
each morning becomes
a silent symphony,
each day is orchestrated
according to the ways of
harmony and peace
and each moment becomes
a sacramental moment
where heaven and earth
have the potential to meet.

Our journey to God
begins afresh each morning.
If we begin the day
in prayer,
in God,
then the day
will flow out
from God
and lead us home
to God.

The Morning Dew

*"The dawn is by its very nature a peaceful, mysterious
time of day – a time when one naturally pauses and looks
with awe at the eastern sky. It is a time of new life, new
beginning and therefore important to the spiritual life: for the
spiritual life is nothing but a perpetual interior renewal."*

—THOMAS MERTON, THE INNER EXPERIENCE *(VII)*

sitting in silence
I hear nothing
and everything

dawn is nice
but too early
too enjoy

the sun rises slowly
and sets too quickly,
leaving me in the dark

five birds swaying
on the telephone line
enjoying the breeze

gentle and loving Mary
full of wonder and grace
gives birth to possibility

The sunrise brings with it a sense of hope. In *Conjectures of a Guilty Bystander,* Merton said it best: "Sunrise is an event that calls forth solemn music in the very depths of man's nature, as if one's whole being has to attune itself to the cosmos and praise God for the new day, praise Him in the name of all the creatures that ever were or ever will be."

July 18, 2010, at 7:22 a.m.: At this moment, I'm seated at my desk and looking out at my garden [in North Hollywood] where the birds are gobbling up the seeds I spread out for them before dawn. The angel on the birdbath and the statue of St. Francis watch in silence. The grass glistens with the morning dew as a blue bird dances about. It is peaceful and calm. It is now, and now is all there is. The calmness and beauty of this moment can easily be lost by useless worry about the future, about what is next now that SDF [the San Damiano Foundation, which was my first film-based ministry] has slipped into the past and is history.

I had no idea when that was written fifteen years ago that Pax et Bonum Communications would rise from the ashes of San Damiano and that in just less than five years I would essentially be living in Haiti and crying babies and gunfire would become the soundtrack of my life. I could not have scripted something so crazy.

The Narrow Path

O God, you know
I want to fulfill
your holy desire
for my life, that I
want to take the path
You wish I would take.
O God, you know also
that I not only stray
from the narrow path
you have chosen for me
but that sometimes
I choose to take
a totally different path.

You, O Lord, are so
gentle and kind.
You give me the freedom
to go the way I wish to go.
But more than that,
You still walk with me,
still love me,
and long to guide me.

Your gift of grace
makes my new path
a new way to You.

You never abandon me
no matter which way I go.
And when I go the wrong way,
a way that would
lead me away from You,
You do not withdraw Your grace
and still gently offer me
opportunities to turn around,
to change my misguided way.
You are a God of endless chances.

Thank you, dear Lord,
for turning my life around.
Please help me
stay on the narrow path
back to Your heart.
Please help me
embrace
more and more of You.

The Still Point

The super-excited,
overstimulated
pace of life today
is way out of sync
with the way
God operates.
God works without
rush or noise
in stillness and silence.

While our lives are lived
in fast-forward,
Christ invites us to
"come apart and rest awhile."
We need to stop running
and find
the still point
where God waits
to embrace us.

A Soothing Ray of Light

O God, help me let go of
everything in my life
and all that I expect and
    wish for.
I know that You have
the best plan for me,
and I am trying
to give You everything:
my life, my time, my possessions,
and my aspirations.
Help me to wait upon You
and not take matters
into my own hands.

I want to give You my all,
and I believe
with all my heart and strength
that You will take care of me,
far and above anything I could
    ever do.
I love you, Lord,
and I want all of my life
to be my gift to You.
Help me, please, dear Lord,
let go of everything
that keeps me from being
more fully united to You.

Lord, help me grow
in humility,
help me to confess
my own brokenness.
Help me move out of my world
of illusion and self-created desires
and into Your universe
of love, joy, and peace.

Lord, I cry out for healing.
Transform my brokenness,
I beg You,
into a new life in You,
the true source
of strength and wholeness.

Help me, Lord, remove everything
that blocks me from joyfully living
the good news of the paschal
    mystery.
O awesome and transcendent
    God,
free me from the slavery of my
    sinfulness.

In my prison of darkness,
Your unmerited grace
is a soothing ray of light.

My Soul is Thirsting for God

My soul has been wounded,
gravely so.
I am unable to heal myself.
You, O God,
alone know the source
of my hidden ailments.
You know all my doubts,
my confusions,
and the endless contradictions
that spring from my meager life.
You know my weaknesses,
my faults,
and my many failures.
You, O God,
alone know
how parched and dry
my inner life is,
how I desperately thirst for the
    only water
that can quench
my intense longing.

I am comforted
that You know
my desire
to know You
more fully,
to love You
more completely.

I truly do want
to be one with You
and to please You always.
But through my fault,
my most grievous fault,
I do not always act
as I wish to act.
I am not always aware
of Your presence
because I am too focused
on myself,
on my own wounds,
my own ideas,
my own selfish desires.
I am bounced around
too easily by
the ideas of others
that appear to sparkle
with truth
yet often are merely
distractions or, worse,
dreadful diversions.
The path to Your door
and the fullness of life
is straight and narrow,
yet I keep veering off
onto cul-de-sacs of
empty promises and
phantom illusions.

My God, my God, Your way is so confusing and hard to follow. Yet it is so clear and so easy to follow. You simply and only want me to love, always, everywhere, everyone. You want me to do as You do, to make myself invisible and silent, to make myself weak and poor, to give myself away, completely and without reservation, so that only You can shine.

In my time of early morning prayer, in the stillness and silence that blankets the coming of dawn, I get it and want to do it. But then I get up, and I am no sooner out of the house, and my resolve begins to dissolve. I argue and become petty. My temper flairs; my joy flees. Resentments rise; faith falls. Doubts and confusions encamp around me. By nightfall, I have been reduced to ashes, a smoldering heap of anguish tormented by my own mediocrity.

But You love me, always, everywhere, even when my behavior turns its back on You.

O my God, I beg You to heal my wounds, to help me go through this day more in harmony with You. Help my faith and actions have smaller and smaller gaps between them. Give me, please, my God, the grace to pause often during the whirlwind of the day, and tell You that I love You, that I need You, that I want to do Your will. Shower the parched, dry, waterless terrain of my inner life with Your abundant grace that will keep You in my heart and mind all day long, especially during those times when I am at my weakest.

I know it is impossible for You to withhold Your love from me. It is the one thing You can't do, for loving is the essence of Your being. Yet all too often, sadly, it is possible for me to reject Your perfect and all-embracing love. I don't mean to reject Your love, for who would reject the most perfect love of all. But I do sometimes forget it, I get distracted or beset by doubts or desires for things not rooted in You. Please, dear Lord, increase Your unmerited grace during those moments of weakness and confusion.

You know and I know that I will fail again. Oh, how that thought pains me. Please continue to reach out Your hand and help me get back up. Without You I am nothing. With You I lack nothing. You are the fullness of life, the fullness of love. In You is endless mercy, endless compassion, endless forgiveness. You alone are holy, You alone are Lord.

Lord, have mercy on me, a lowly sinner.

I Hand It All to You

Oh my God, help me
to stop picking away at
the sore of my guilt
over my past misdeeds,
the many times
I failed to love.
Help me instead
To fix my gaze on
Your endless love.
Help me see
how my sins
are merely manifestations
of my own inner emptiness
and an indication of
how far I am from You,
the true source of love.

I give you, my God,
everything that is
within me.
I also surrender
all of my past.
I hand it all to You
and accept your
total forgiveness,
your overflowing mercy,
and your boundless love.

I also give You
all the wounds
life has inflicted on me.
Give me, please,

the grace
to look at them honestly,
to feel them fully,
and then entrust them
to your Divine care.
Help me also forgive
all who have harmed me,
and allow me
to forget the painful memories
that only allow the harm to live.

This day, I see my past,
my faults,
my wounds,
my shame . . .
and I let them go.
I give them to You.
I seek your Spirit
in order to have
the faith and strength
to live fully
in the present day,
consciously aware of
each precious, life-giving
moment.

A Journey to Weakness

The emptiness I often feel
stems from not realizing
I am made for communion
with You.
If I am not growing
toward unity with You,
my God,
then I am growing
apart from You.
Help me learn to be still,
to be humble,
to move into
a greater union
with You.
Only in stillness and humility
can I enter a dialogue with You,
sweet Jesus.
I need to bring to You
what I am
so that in time
I might become
more like
what You are.

In following you,
Lord Jesus,
I have seen
with my own eyes
in so many places
around the world
how life is filled
to overflowing
with pain and struggle.

Your way leads to
the Cross,
and it doesn't offer
an easy way
around it.
To become Your disciple
means accepting
a spirituality of
the Cross
and renouncing
a spirituality of glory.

*O God, help me follow wherever
    You lead me.*

I believe my spiritual life
is essentially a journey
in which I move from
what I am
to what I will become.
I am just beginning to learn
that life is a journey
to weakness.
The saints truly learned
to live
when they began
to explore
their own weaknesses.
By Your unmerited grace,
every experience
of weakness
is an opportunity
of growth and renewed life.

Weaknesses transformed by
the reality of Christ's love
become life-giving virtues.

You humbled Yourself
to love me.

You gave of Yourself
to love me.
Help me give myself
to love You
and all of creation.

In the Desert

At some point in time,
God calls each of us
into the desert.
The desert is
a place of discipline,
which we need
but don't want,
and so we avoid it.
In the desert,
under the blazing sun,
all our weaknesses
are made clear.
We look around
and see
the vastness of nothing.
We do not know
which way to go.
In the desert,
our need for God
is also made clear.

In the desert,
we grow weary;
we lose hope.

We can't quench
our own thirst;
we know no pleasure.
All around is only a void
that stretches out
beyond our sight.
The day turns to night.

The arid, parched landscape
can only be watered by God.
God's water is sweet;
God's manna is tasty.
In the desert,
God's love is
our only comfort.
In the desert,
God's spirit transcends
the bleakness
in the depths of our souls
and we can see
beauty and tenderness.
In the desert,
ideas about God
give way to God.

O Lord, help me not evade the desert, not flee the pain of life, the suffering that not even Your beloved Son avoided. Help me enter the desert of silence, the desert of surrender, the desert of doubt, the desert of sorrow and loneliness so I can be nourished by Your loving Word alone, which is the only source of true refreshment and lasting peace.

Between Night and Day

As each new day dawns,
God's light gives us
a renewed pledge
of God's love,
a fresh beginning
that is pure gift,
a gift meant to be
given away
during the day.
In the silence between
night and day,
I feel God's grace and peace
and am commissioned
to become
an instrument
of that very same
grace and peace.
In the splendor of
new light,
God's love and mercy
are revealed.

O God, help me to see the radiance of Your light and show me this day how to be a servant of Your peace. Help me, O God, to share the delicate, intoxicating fragrance of Your mercy and love with those whose lives are lived on the shadowy and dismal margins, with those whose days see no happiness, with those whose days end without hope.

First and Foremost

O Lord, my mind and heart
are centered on
so many things
other than You.
Mostly good things,
but not You.
Help me this day
to desire You
first and foremost,
and not to be distracted
by all the things that
pull me this way and that way,
fragmenting my being.
Teach me this day, O Lord,
how to forget
my fears and anxieties,
and put all my trust and hope
in You alone.

O God, You know
my plans.
Help me hear
Your plan
for me.
Help me know
when my plans
are rooted in
my false self,
the "me" that does not see
its own weakness and pride.
Help me never forget
that the only bread I need
is You.

Present Moment

"I Am," says God.
God did not say,
"I Was," or
"I Will Be."
In saying, "I Am,"
God is saying,
"I am present."

Am *I* present?
Or do I live in the past,
replaying old scenes,
clinging to old wounds?

Am I present?
Or do I live in the future,
chained to useless fantasies
and baseless fears?

God is beyond time
and always present.
But we look away.
We look back
and are hurt.
We look ahead
and are terrorized.
In this present moment,
God is facing us.
In this present moment,
we will no longer be
victims of the past or
be paralyzed by the future.
In this present moment
we can face God.
In this present moment
we can encounter God.

*Oh God, help me be
in this present moment.
Oh God, help me see
in this present moment
You.
Oh God, help me see You
in all I do,
in all my encounters,
in all the people I meet,
in all of creation.*

Bitter Cross

O sweet Lord,
I want so very much
to avoid the bitter cross
You ask me to carry,
the cross of putting aside
    everything
that is outside the realm
of Your love.
Actually, nothing is outside
the realm of Your love,
because You so long for us,
so thirst for us,
that You follow us into
the darkest corners
of our lives, looking
to embrace us
with Your mercy and compassion.
Yet I so often want
to embrace things

that You find unhealthy
and unfitting
for a seeker of God.

O Lord, help me see,
feel, and know
that outside of You
there is nothing of any worth,
and that with You
all is priceless.
Help me nail to the cross
the secret things
in my heart
that I must sacrifice
to follow You
more closely
and love You
more dearly.

A More Suitable Chamber

O Lord, help me to renew
my innermost being.
I stumble and fall often.
My many failures
disappoint me.
But You
never treat me
as I deserve.
You close Your eyes
to my faults.

I trust in Your
endless mercy
and compassion.
Still, I need Your help
to truly purify
my deepest being,
to create there
a more suitable chamber
for Your spirit
to reside.

Endless Love

You alone, my God,
are faithful
to your promises.
I know You are with me,
walking beside me,
and I have no reason
to fear or doubt . . .

but I am weak
and need Your strong arm.
I appeal to Your gentleness,
O God of mercy.
I seek Your Divine help,
O God of compassion.
I cling to Your faithfulness,
O God of endless love.

My Refuge

God you have been
my refuge
from year to year;
You are my refuge
from day to day,
even from hour to hour.
Blessed are you, Lord.
Show me, I beg,
what You want me to do,
who You want me
to become.
I am Yours.
Yet, I still need to learn
Your will,
learn what You desire
for me,
for You are my God.
You are the source
and sustainer
of all life.
Yet I still stray from You.
You are the only light
to lead me out of
my own darkness.
Lord, have mercy
on me,
a sinner.

The Canvas of My Soul

Oh God, I have not yet
truly begun to paint
the canvas of my soul.
Help me find
the vivid brushstrokes
of love, tenderness,
compassion, wonder,
poetry, and purity
needed to create
a portrait inspired by
You to be given as a gift
to all who see it.

Help me replace
the dark, hidden tones
of my life
with the numinous hues
that reveal harmony and balance.
Have the borders of my canvas
not be so small
as to exclude
the richness and diversity
of all humanity
and the endless paths
to the Divine.

Lord, hear my plea,
be mindful of my cry.
Help me cleanse
all traces of deceitfulness
within me
so my prayer may reach
your ear.

Lord, show me the path
to the truth and beauty
of your loving heart.
Help me search
my wounded heart
for unloving tendencies.

Show Me the Way

Lord God,
I give You permission
to be the Lord of my life
and the Lord of my ministry.
You, Lord,
are the creator and sustainer
of the universe,
yet You have no power
over my life
unless I allow You
to help me.
You are all powerful
and yet You are
a God of poverty
out of respect for
my free will.
You give me,
a weak pauper,
the power
to say yes or no
to the abundance of grace
You wish to shower on me
every moment of my life.

Every day,
in countless small ways,
I mount the throne of my life
and make myself
the lord of my life.

I say You are Lord,
but I do not relinquish
my throne.
I do things my way.
Your way is often
an untaken path.

You want to be
the Lord of my life.
Not because
You like being Lord,
or need or want to be Lord.
You want to be the Lord
of my life
because You know
that is what is best for me.
And because You love me
You only want
what is best for me.

O my God,
I am tired of
being lord of my life.
My way is a dead end.
Your way leads to eternal life.
O my God, I give You permission
to be the Lord of my life.
Show me the way.
Amen.

Bowing is an integral part
of Eastern Christianity . . .
bowing before icons
and the Eucharistic presence.
Bowing is expression of
spiritual humility,
which directs our hearts toward
the unseen Divine.
In bowing, we affirm
Christ's transformative capacity
to help us become
more loving and
more merciful.
Bowing is difficult
when our heart is
weary or broken,
but that is the best time
to bow to the
God of creation and peace
as our silent physical gesture
for help in restoring
a heart that beats
in harmony with
Christ's all-loving heart.

The Spring in My Step

Jesus,
you are the light
in my darkness.
You are the hope
in my despair.

Jesus,
you bring joy
to my sadness
You bring clarity
to my confusion.

Jesus,
you bring laugher
to my tears.
You bring answers
to my questions.

Jesus,
you bring calmness
to my restlessness.
You bring presence
to my loneliness.

Jesus,
you are the spring
in my step.
You bring direction
to my wanderings.

PART THREE

Scribbled Thoughts

You need to put
yourself
in a place
where
grace can
flow
to you.

See the reality
of this
moment.

Experiencing pain
opens the heart
to grow in
compassion
for others and
all of creation.
Out of sorrow
we awake to
a new experience of
humor and joy.

You cannot become
fully human
without helping
others to become
fully human.

The spiritual life
has more to do
with subtraction
than addition.

The presence
of God
is found in
the absence
of things
not of God.

So much of life is
contradiction and chaos.
Only in stillness and prayer
can harmony emerge
from the confusion.

In stillness
we detect
the movement
of God.

In stillness
we feel
the movement
of God's Spirit
transforming our hearts.

We seek to make
connections.
God calls us into
communion.

Within everyone we meet
there is an inherent
goodness.
It is our duty
to shine a light
on that goodness.

To not love
your enemies
is to believe
they are beyond
the scope of
God's power.

Every facet of our lives
needs to be permeated
by love
to grow closer
to God.
Any portion of our lives
that we have not surrendered
to love
becomes an obstacle
to reaching God.

Fluency
in biblical exegesis
is not
holiness.

The size of a church
is not an indication of
the truth it contains.

Faith requires
a passion for
the truth.

How do I
reach out
to others
without being
pulled down
by them?

The danger of our thirst
for individualism is that
it weakens our awareness
of the needs of others.
From Christ's point of view,
"you" comes before "me."

Acknowledging my own weakness
increases my ability
to become
more merciful toward others.

The widespread existence of hunger
is a massive violation
of human rights
bordering on
epidemic proportions.

We are all outraged
when human rights
are violated by terrorism,
repression, and murder.
But where is the outrage
when human rights
are violated by
the existence of dire conditions
of extreme poverty
and unjust economic structures
that give rise to vast inequalities?

To learn the causes of poverty,
we must spend time with the poor.
If we share in their struggles,
we can share in their liberation.

The essence of Christ's message is:
Make every stranger,
no matter how poor or dirty,
no matter how weak or unlovable,
your neighbor.
Tough message.

To turn your back
on the poor
is to turn your back
on Jesus.

Relinquishing
the possessions
of the ego
we all amass
inside ourselves
is the most demanding
form of poverty.

True poverty
is total trust
in God.

The greatest violation of poverty
is to hold on to
the good God gives—
goodness must flow.

Jesus invited
the poor and the outcasts
to sit at his banquet table.
Who are our dinner guests?

Giving food to the poor is easy.
Eating with the poor is much harder . . .
and much more rewarding.
Jesus ate with the poor,
and He asks us to do the same.
Communion with the poor is
an enriching source of healing.

Acts of charity are
the wings of Love.

God's love
excludes no one.

Finding holiness
requires finding
yourself.

The garden of solitude
produces many beautiful flowers,
the most beautiful of which
is compassion.

There is no time—
there is only
the ever-present now.

The blending of
the inspirational and
the incarnational
creates a holistic spirituality.

Stillness, silence,
and solitude
form a triptych
of the holy life.

Humility, detachment,
charity, and compassion
are the cornerstones
of the Christian life.

The essence of all creation
is the glorification of God:
"Holy, holy, holy, Lord of Sabaoth.
Heaven and earth
are full of thy glory."

The poor, the weak, and the hurting are God made visible.

While the prosperous around the world
are sipping bottled spring water,
nearly two million people living in poverty
are forced to drink and bathe in water contaminated
with deadly parasites and pathogens.

Consuming more than you need
is stealing from those in need.

As long as we enjoy comfort
and require security,
it will be
impossible to have
true compassion for
the poor and the weak.

The poor taught me
to see
the barrenness of affluence
and
the emptiness of consumerism.

We find it more comfortable
to put limits on God,
and in doing so
we create a spiritual poverty
within us.

We must become
the poor Christ . . .
offered up
and
given away.

Only when I am vulnerable
is it possible for me
to be broken
and restored
to the image of God.

Breaking the bondage
of egoism
is the toughest task
in life.

Liberation is
difficult and painful.

In the state of
emptiness,
you are better able
to encounter the
fullness
of God.

To become poor
in spirit
is to know
the richness
of God.

Poverty of spirit
frees us
from the tyranny
of wealth.

Love is
the only antidote
to selfishness.

Acts of love
give flesh to
faith and hope.

Simplicity immunizes you
from the plague of
consumerism.

Justice should compel us
to meet the needs of
the poor.

If you want to show
gratitude
to God,
be generous
to others.

The virtue of poverty
is that it leads one
to recognize that
God alone
can provide us
with what we
truly need.

Giving a few dollars
to the poor
is not the same
as being one
with the poor,
which is what
Christ requires.

My awareness of
God's mysterious presence
within me
makes me more aware of
the same presence
within others.

Jesus embraced,
touched, and loved
the poor, the outcasts,
and the rejected.
He called them
"blessed."
For Jesus,
the poor and lowly
are sacraments,
because they offer
a direct way
to encounter God.

We can discover
our true selves
only through
the sincere gift
of ourselves.

The despised and
the unimportant of
the world
are loved unconditionally
by their Creator.

Both the New and
the Old Testament
reveal God's
preferential love
for those the world
ignores and rejects.

Although God's love embraces
all people,
God has clearly demonstrated
deep concern
for the poor and the needy,
the helpless and the oppressed.
God demands that we
side with the poor, the powerless,
and the victims of injustice.
To walk with the poor
is to be in harmony with
the will of God.

Oh God, in your
merciful goodness,
forgive us
the polarities and prejudices
we have created and accepted
within the human family,
which you created
to live in peace,
unity, and harmony.

By loving the poor
and insignificant
first and foremost,
God demonstrates
the extent and fullness
of Divine love
for all of creation.

Poverty touches Mother Earth also—when we take without regard to the consequences of our actions. To pollute our rivers, to strip our mountains of their trees, to fill the air with deadly toxins is to impoverish future generations. Love and justice demand we treat earth as our sister, to nurture and protect her. St. Francis of Assisi, who heard nature sing God's glory, reminds us that all creation is related and must live in communion. Every time an aspect of creation is disrespected, we lose another connection with the Creator.

God hides
in a piece of
broken bread
and in the
broken life
of a slum-dweller.

God wants us
to see each other
as tabernacles,
as secret hiding places
for the Divine.
Pray for the grace
to be able to see
a homeless person
as a tabernacle of God.

Action is as important
as prayer;
each of us must
take responsibility
for meeting the world's need,
for we are the
accomplices of evil
if we do nothing
to prevent it.

In condemning others,
we avoid the more difficult task
of knowing ourselves.

The lack of jobs and
long-term unemployment
that plagues the urban slums
increases the social isolation
of the inner-city poor.

The life of Christ
illustrates that
forgiveness and charity
should have no limits.

Unconditional mercy
requires total forgiveness
with absolutely no conditions.
To place conditions
on mercy and forgiveness
is a form of violence.

At its root,
there is only one reason
for the existence of poverty:
selfishness,

which is a manifestation
of a lack of
authentic love.

We all crave to be
on the receiving end
of a gift of love,
but our very craving masks
a deeper, more profound
human need:
to give love.

Poverty isn't just a matter of not having sufficient income to live. Poverty isn't just living with hunger. The poor also experience a total lack of a sense of well-being and peace of mind, which so many of us take for granted. Poverty isn't about the lack of food, shelter, and security; poverty is the rage one feels when you can't do anything about it. Poverty is the sense of hopelessness that kills the spirit.

The spiritual life does not lift us out of the human condition, with its misery, problems, confrontations, pain, and difficulties. Oh, but if it did. Spiritual life plunges us more deeply into our humanity. It would be nice to sit in church all day, our hands clasped in prayer, drinking in the ecstasy of the Lord. But that is unrealistic; we must enter into the marketplace, walk the alleys of commerce. We must help each other out of the ditches we fall into. It is in the streets of life that we encounter God. Everything human is Divine.

For St. Francis of Assisi,
the essential ingredient of
Gospel poverty is
"living without grasping."
For most of us today,
our lives are marked by
a hunger to grab all we can.

The greedy tendencies
of the ego
and its insatiable hunger
for possessions
robs us of our wholeness.
We become whole again
when the self learns how
to be empty,
willing to lose itself
in order to enter into
a deep and rich communion
with others.
Community is
the womb of love.
In community,
love is planted, nurtured,
and birthed.

We must all work
to create a society
that is founded on
welcome and respect,
embracing the most vulnerable
among us.

God's mercy is
expressed through
other people.
We are called to be
conduits of mercy.

Jesus instructed us
to never think of ourselves
as more important than others,
to never put ourselves
before anyone.
His message is clear:
Think little of yourself
and be happy
that others do not consider
you very important.
Moreover, Jesus asks us
to stop struggling to
control events
for our own benefit
and instead try to be
a servant to others.

God loves us because
we are weak and powerless,
not in spite of those qualities.
We need to accept
that we are all
poor and needy,
and that only God
can lift us up.

In our encounters with the poor,
we must move from
pity to love,
from charity to justice.

The seduction of possessions
blinds us
to the needs of the poor.

When profit is
the aim and law of life,
then humanity
suffers a great loss.

The road to God
is straight and narrow.
The road is poverty.
We must be willing
to go to God
with empty hands,
trusting God
for everything.

The world demands
more and more
from us.
God only asks for
empty hands.

The Cries of God

We pray for our daily bread.
Yet for millions of people around the world,
their daily bread consists of
violence, famine, and destruction.

Did God hear our prayer and not theirs?

No.

God hears the cries of the poor.
We do not hear the cries of God
asking us to be Divine hands
tending to the needs of the poor.

God took on human form
as a vulnerable baby,
the child of homeless refugees,
needing human help
in the ongoing work of creation.
We are God's messengers
delivering food and hope
to those living with hunger and death.

We are all called,
no matter our faith
or lack of faith,
to become instruments of
peace, mercy, and compassion
because in the stunning
diversity of humanity,
there are no others:
we are one . . .
different but the same.

The face of God
is so vast
it is faceless
from our limited
perspective.
The great fifteenth-century
German mystic
Nicholas of Cusa taught,
"Every face you encounter in life
is a face of the Faceless One."

We are all part of
the infinite reality
that is the face of God,
each of us are like
little bits of colored tile
in the vast mosaic
that is the Divine face,
each of us a tiny part
of the infinite reality
that is the Divine face.

Each of us
is a sacred
and complex
unity of
body, soul,
and mind.

There is a sense
that the old certainties
that held things together
can no longer be
a guarantee of
whatever passes
as normal.

Today the world has become
disenchanted.
In the marketplace
of life today
souls and Spirit
are excluded.

We hunger for something
bigger and better
than consumption
and the monotony of
modern existence.
We long for
a renewal of our
connection to God.

For the most part,
we live in a world
of our own making.
We hunger for
a more meaningful life,
yet we keep looking for
more prestige and possessions,
trapped in mindless
consumption.

In the malaise of
modernity,
we feel vulnerable,
yet we feel and wish for
a more meaningful
life.

God is absent
in modern life,
or on a long
vacation.

Religious art
and Gregorian chant
keeps me
afloat
in the wreckage
of modern life.

I live with my doubts.
My longing for God
is occasionally dulled by
uncertainty.
My hope is riddled
with questions.

Rabbi Michael Learner said,
"To be in real connection
to God
is to be in
awe and amazement
at the universe
that God created."

Rabbi Abraham Josuha Heschel taught,
"Prayer begins at the edge of emptiness."

I was happy
to discover
someone
who greatly admired
the great Jewish rabbi
Abrahm Joshua Heschel
as much as I do.

My fellow admirer
said that Heschel claimed,
*Every human being
had a binary choice
to make:
pursue pleasure
or
serve God.*

*"All the wise have said the same:
The one who knows God
is God's mercy to His creatures."*

—RUMI

*"Everything that is in the heavens,
on earth, and under the earth
is penetrated with connectedness,
penetrated with relatedness."*

—HILDEGARD OF BINGEN

*"There will be no lasting peace on earth
unless we learn not merely to tolerate
but even to respect the other faiths as our own.
A reverent study of the sayings
of different teachers of humanity
is a step in the direction of such mutual respect."*

—MAHATMA GANDHI

*"Your life is shaped by the end you live for. You
are made in the images of what you desire."*

—THOMAS MERTON, THOUGHTS IN SOLITUDE

"We are already one. But we imagine that we are not. And what we have to recover is our original unity. What we have to be is what we are."

—THOMAS MERTON, *THE ASIAN JOURNAL*

It is essential
that humanity learns
to live in
a symbiotic relationship
with nature.

PART FOUR

A Mystical Force

A Loving Embrace

If you have the Trinity
figured out,
you have accomplished
the impossible.

The Triune God is
a dynamic . . .
a dynamic love relationship,
changing, growing, deepening.

The Trinity doesn't simply live
in unchanging truths;
the Trinity lives
in a loving embrace of creation.

*"When I see your heavens,
the work of your hands,
the moon and stars
that you put in place—
what are we
that you are mindful of us?"*
—Psalm 8

Designed to Be Shared

To think of God
outside the context of
love and community
is not to think about God.
For God is love,
and God's love,
as illustrated in the Trinity,
is communal,
designed to be shared
with all
and without exception.

Riding an Ox

Way back in the fourteenth century, Meister Eckhart employed a metaphor first used by the Buddhists: "I was a man riding an ox looking for an ox to ride on." For many years, I was looking for God until I finally reached the point where I had to quit looking and start realizing.

Grace is God's way
of talking to us.
We can best experience grace
and therefore hear God
more clearly
when we stop
living for ourselves
and instead give ourselves
in loving service
to others.

Drumbeat

The loud drumbeat of
fear and anxiety
can be quieted by
contemplation.

When Christ reveals
His heart to us,
He also reveals
our sinfulness.

The deadliest characteristic
of sin
is its ease
of repetition.

God does not seek
perfection in us.
God wants
repentance.

Jesus does not promise
happiness.
He proclaims the
beatitudes.

A Love Affair

God loves us
as we are,
not as
we should be.

Christianity is not
a moral code—
it is a love affair.

We are supposed to be
human torches
ignited by
the furious, flaming
love of God.

Endless Mercy

In our frailty
and weaknesses,
in our doubts
and confusion,
God is still
at home,
still with us.
God's love
knows our struggles
and failures ...
and wants to shower us
with mercy.

I can't hide
my many screw-ups
from God.
I can only
surrender them
to God.
My "sins" are
only deadly
if I fail
to let go of them
and surrender them
to God's endless mercy.

Unique and Special

So much loss
of life
by violence
in Haiti.
Senseless violence.
Cruel violence.
When one life
is lost
someone completely
unique
is gone . . .
forever.
This is a tragedy
beyond measure.

Every life
is unique
and special
in the eyes of
God.

Over 5,000 Haitians
were killed
by barbaric
gang violence
in 2024.

Shameful.
The lost presence
of those slaughtered
people
created a tidal wave
of tears and
inconsolable grief.

Those slain souls
were expendable
and worthless
in the bloodthirsty
eyes of the gangs.
But they were
of eternal worth
to God.

When will the senseless
violence end?
When more and more
of us begin
to attune our hearts,
our eyes, our ears
to the God of
love and peace.

A Journey Toward Understanding

Interfaith dialogue requires
that people of differing faiths
avoid dogmatic assertions
when speaking with each other.
Theological arrogance and rigidity
stifles any authentic exchange.
Nor will dialogue succeed
if our aim is selling
our theological perspective.
True dialogue requires an honest
mutual exploration
of our respective theologies
and felt experiences of God;
it a journey toward
understanding,
not convincing.

Perhaps people of
differing faiths
can each grow
closer to God
by drawing
closer to each other.

The path of peace
is dialogue.
Dialogue transforms
a stranger into a friend.
Friends can unite
in the struggle against
poverty and evil.

The world's faiths speak
in uniquely different tongues
of a transcendent reality
common to them all.

The Wonder of Creation

Our senses have become
dulled
to the wonder
of creation,
which it takes
for granted.

Technical skill and
tangible results,
high priests of our age,
are of little worth
in the spiritual life,
which places a premium on
integrity and integration.

The mystery of life
cannot be solved
with scientific or
psychological answers.
The key to the solution,
if there even is one,
is mystical.

The eternal confounds
everything we say
and do.

Life is littered with
conflicts
that cannot be
resolved.

A Field of Poppies

Our spirits need
time to rest,
to wander in
a field of poppies,
to soar with
the sunrise,
to swing in
a hammock,
to jump into
a lake.
Our spirits need time
to simply do
nothing,
which, oddly enough,
will give us the ability
to do everything better.

Solitude gives us
insight
into our deepest
needs and feelings.

Tranquility of
heart and mind
springs naturally
from the well
of solitude.
God speaks
in silence.

An Oasis of Silence

True silence is
a garden enclosed,
where alone the soul
can meet its God.

Silence is a gift
from God,
to let us speak
more intimately
with God.
If you are constantly talking,
God will be unable
to teach you anything.

If you don't listen,
you will never learn.

A free moment
is a moment free
to speak to God.

Prayer essentially is
loving God,
which is why
we need to deepen
our prayer life
to deepen our love.

Fifteen centuries ago, in a time of great uncertainty and social change, St. Benedict, the father of Western monasticism, wrote a rule for his monks, which stressed the balance between prayer and work. Serve your brother, Benedict advised, while you seek God. Benedict believed a person's most basic inclination and need was to seek God, and so he insisted a monk's day have sufficient time for private meditative reading and prayer.

We need to spend less time
trying to understand God
and more time adoring God.

When freed from merely
mouthing petitions,
prayer expands our
self-knowledge and consciousness.
Once the clouds of
self-deception have been
blown away by prayer,

the need for repentance
becomes clear:
We are not who, or how,
we once thought we were.
When an understanding
of who we are
and where we came from
permeates our entire being,
we are truly on the road
to redemption.

We each need to create
our own sacred space,
a space outside the rat race,
an oasis of silence,
a space dedicated to inwardness,
a simple space of
sanity and sanctity.
We can turn any space
into a sacred space.
A bedroom corner

can be a basilica,
a portal into the mystery
and meaning of life.

All of creation calls us
to be present . . .
to the beauty of creation,
to the sounds of the birds,
to the wonder of the sunrise,
to the night sanctuaries of silence.

The Bottom Line

Prayer stimulates
a mindfulness of God,
which in turn stimulates
acts of love and mercy.

Love is service.
It is the emptying of self.
It is losing in order to find.

Acknowledging my own weakness
increases my ability
to be more merciful toward
    others.

The Christian life
can be reduced to this:
Live the beatitudes.

Bird Watching

Beauty is
everywhere.
Every landscape
we love is
the landscape
of our soul.

Pay attention
to the lilies;
watch
the birds.

Celebrate life . . .
instead of trying
to control it.

Your Neighbor's Yard

The faults of my neighbor
must be of no concern to me
nor be the subject of my idle chatter,
whose only purpose is to spotlight
my virtuousness and flatter my ego.

Let words fly from your mouth
on the gentle yet strong
wings of humility.

Goodness, from a Christian perspective,
does not come from morality
but from communion
with God and neighbor.

The path to God
runs through
your neighbor's yard.

A Faint Echo

We were created
in, by, and through
love.
We were made
for intimacy
with God.

Intimacy with God
is at the heart
of all our searching
for human friendship and
     intimacy.
We become more fully human
only in relationship
to our ever-deepening
consciousness of
and abandonment to
God,
the true source of
fulfillment and love.

Happiness and peace
is found
in a self-emptying love
that is made tangible
in a relationship
with another.

Happiness and peace
are not found
in isolation.
We are communal beings,

the fruit of
communal love
made tangible
within the loving exchange
found in the triune God.

Human love is merely
a faint echo
of Divine love.
Human love is
weak, imperfect, and
prone to failure
because of our
ingrained selfishness.

But every loving
human relationship,
no matter how flawed,
teaches us—
if we are open and willing to
     learn—
about the constantly beckoning,
always giving,
ever deepening,
perpetually self-emptying
love of God.

Love is not merely
romance.
Love is a school
where you learn
to let go

of all that is not God
so you can be filled
with God.

When two become
one flesh,
they begin to sense
the beautiful unity
of God
and begin to take
feeble steps toward
true self-emptying intimacy
for which each of us
was created.

We have turned
the words
"I love you"
into a trite expression
—spoken today,
forgotten tomorrow—
but they are the most
powerful words
we can ever utter.
We long to hear those words,
words that God whispers
every day.

The Beauty of All Life

We are slow
to compassion
because we are quick
to exploit
others for
our own gain.

As we grow in compassion
we are able to see more clearly
the beauty of all life,
and we also increase our desire
to transform everything ugly
into something beautiful.

Given Away

The best way
to lovingly serve
our neighbor
is to take our eyes off
ourselves,
to forget ourselves,
to become unimportant
to ourselves,
and fix our eyes and hearts
and minds on Christ.
We must let go of
self-centeredness
to love with true purity
under all circumstances.

Justice should be
moved by love
to meet the needs
of the poor.

The emerging global economy
has a strong tendency to foster
soulless consumerism and
mindless worship
of technology,
and it often tramples the rights
of workers and the poor.
We need to be attentive

to the human consequences
and social impact
of globalization.

We must become
the poor Christ . . .
offered up
and given away.

Both the New and the Old
    Testament
reveal God's preferential love
for those the world ignores
    and rejects.

The despised and the
    unimportant
of the world
are loved unconditionally
by their Creator.

By loving the poor and
    insignificant
first and foremost,
God demonstrates
the extent and fullness
of Divine love
for all of creation.

Not So Amazing Grace

God's grace isn't often
easy to see.
Heck . . . it not even
easy to define.
Speaking about pornography,
someone once said they
couldn't define it
but they would know it
if they saw it.
It seems we don't really
see grace
except in retrospect . . .
long after the fact.

Grace is really not
so amazing;
grace is commonplace . . .
grace is happening
all the time,
all around us,
because God is
always present.

True Freedom

Humanity tends to
view greatness
in relation to
one's ability to
dominate.
Jesus offers
a different perspective.
For Him,
greatness lies
in the ability
to give oneself
away.

The wonder of
the universe
and the totality of
our humanity
is within ourselves.
It is a
gift of life

that we must
give away
in order to
possess it.

To be in
communion
with God
and each other
we must liberate
ourselves
from ourselves,
from our hungry
egos
in order to be
free enough
to give ourselves
to the Other
and each other.

The Cross of Love

I have always been drawn
to the Cross,
normally through
paintings and icons.
But I found the theology
behind the images
to be problematic.

After walking poverty road
through many slums
around the world
for a quarter century,
I see the crucifixion of Christ
as the ultimate example
of self-emptying
more than as
the key to salvation.
Christ died on the cross
to teach us a lesson:
Love demands sacrifice
and is often painful.

This, of course, marks me as a heretic.

Cathedrals of the Poor

The slums of Kampala (in Uganda)
are the kind of places
where I come
when I really want to
commune with God,
a place where ramshackle huts
are stained-glass windows of
    heaven
through which the
light of God
pours through.
For me, the far-too-numerous
and massive slums
that dot the landscape of
so many developing nations
are Cathedrals of the Poor,
places so real and raw
that they pulsate
with the presence of God.
In these slums,
you are on holy ground
because Jesus is here
in the form of people
suffering from hunger and
curable diseases.

Christ wants us to live
a life of detachment
and expectation.
But we cling
to the countless things
we think are important.

We chase after
what we don't have;
we lust after
what is beyond our reach.
We have turned greed and
    hoarding
into virtues.
Consumed by our need
for comfort and security,
we have become blinded
to the needs of the poor.
We do not share,
and our selfishness
is the cause of
much of the poverty
we see.

Economic policies
in affluent nations
often have a devastating impact
on destitute people
living in destitute countries,
making basic human dignity
something that is
far beyond their reach.
The people in the slums of
    Kampala
have no voice,
no power,
no rights . . . and no way
to make their plight known.

We are driven by
economic success.
We worship on the altar
of consumerism.
Christ showed us
a different way—
a way of simplicity,
dependence upon God
and extending good will
to others.

Our commodity economy
is not in harmony
with the teachings of Jesus.
We need to share our time,
our treasure,
our love
with the chronically poor.
Jesus wants us
to give our lives away.
This is Gospel giving.

The Cries of the Poor

The cries of the poor
and the oppressed,
the very stench
of their unjust deaths,
has been met by
a heartless indifference
that amounts to nothing less
than cruel inhumanity.

In a world of wealth,
the poor live in
an endless *Shoah,*
living on pennies a day,
dying hungry and alone
at night. Forced displacement,
unemployment, exclusion,
isolation, rejection,
starvation,
no permanent home,
no sewage,
no access to clean water
and medical care . . .
these are the harsh,
menacing realities
faced by the acutely poor.
Their corpses are piling high,
thousands upon thousands a day,
all victims of
our insensitivity and apathy.

Where is the indignation?
Where is the compassion?
We have lost our sense
of mercy,
lost our sense
of connectedness.
It is easy to blame
the corrupt governments
that imprison the poor
in massive slums;
it is harder to raise
our voices in protest,
to cry out for
the rights of the marginalized.

Whether implicitly or explicitly,
we all seek security and
    consolation.
Yet even when we find
some level of security,
some degree of consolation,
it isn't enough.
For many, security and
    consolation
are beyond their reach.
Far beyond.
Jesus claimed that
true security and consolation
could only be found in God.

That was mostly written in Uganda. In 2008 and 2009, I made three grueling trips to Uganda to a make a film tilted The Fragrant Spirit of Life. *After the film was released, Harcourt Religion, which distributed the film, commissioned a study guide to be written. I was asked to submit a brief statement about the film. With minor changes, here it is:*

> The experience of making this film—as well as traveling to and living in the worst slums in nine nations over an 18-month period beginning in 2000)—forever changed me. I've seen scenes from *The Fragrant Spirit of Life* hundreds of times during my presentations in high schools and colleges across the nation, and every time I see the scenes, I am pushed to the verge of tears and challenged by my own words. The film is uncompromising and relentlessly hard. I am still struggling to live the truth I discovered in these dreadful places. But this I know for sure: I am eternally grateful for the lessons I learned from the poor and I pray that I shall never forget my own true poverty and my need for God.
>
> While some of the images in the film are tough to look at (especially the two naked kids—Sam and Esther—lying in the dirt who were starving and immobilized by polio), they are, however, not meant to make you feel downcast or ashamed or guilty. I am not interested in shaming anyone into helping the poor. I simply want to show you their life, a life lived without the basic essentials we take for granted. In these slums, I saw the hands and feet of Jesus nailed to scrap wood over and over and over again. But I was surprised to discover that the agony of poverty and violence did not still the Spirit in the souls of most of the people. The fragrant spirit of life smiles through the pain of living and the mystery of death. This is my plea: Visit the poor, sit with them, talk with them, be one with them. This is my prayer: *O come, breathe in the Spirit, exhale the Love, give birth to faith and hope.*

In the Belly of the Beast

This was written in the summer of 2015, and tweaked a few times over the years. This latest version was finished on June 2, 2025, in a guesthouse in the woods in Monterey, Massachusetts, while in exile from Haiti.

To be in Haiti
is to be in
the belly of
the beast.
In Haiti,
the presence of God takes
on the form of absence.
It is the sign of Jonah
writ large.

In Haiti
human misery is
raw and real.
In Haiti
I saw things
in their utter nakedness.
The Cross was
around every corner.
The Cross had
no place to hide.
I had to close my eyes
to the Cross or
I had to confront
and embrace the Cross.

In Haiti
my false ideas
and values
were shattered into
thousands of little pieces.
I saw clearly
the pain and suffering
of Christ,
the pain and suffering
of the human condition.

In Haiti there are
no diversions,
no false idols
to avert my gaze
from the misery.
There was no place to turn . . .
all I could see was
the hiddenness of God,
the apparent absence of God.
In this void
I slowly and humbly
prepared to approach
the consciousness of God.
In the absence of God,
the presence of God awaits.
Detachment, for me,
seemed to be
the path to wholeness.

In the slums of Haiti,
I felt closer to God
than I do at
Sunday Mass
in my home parish.
In Haiti, I was detached
from the world
yet not attached
to God.
It was a place
of dreadful inner anguish
for me.

I could neither believe
nor not believe
in anything.
Yet, somehow in Haiti
I felt God
was hidden in
the insignificant
and the unassuming,
like Christ hiding
in a morsel of bread.

The poor felt
their own fragility
and understood
their own dependency.
In Haiti I felt
the way to God
was through the misery
and nothingness
of my false self.
In Haiti I saw
more clearly
my true self
and my complete
dependence upon God.
It is in Haiti
that I feel more tangibly
God's love.

Love is a mystical force
that pushes open
the door to
forgiveness and mercy.

Pain and Suffering

Unmindful consumption
is a sure path
to suffering.

By moving through
and beyond suffering
we enter the freedom
of God.

In silence, we become
aware that we may have
wandered off the path
to the inner freedom
produced by
a God-centered life.
In silence, we turn around
and find our way back
to the true path.

In silence, we can hear
our inner cravings
and recognize the pain
caused by our separation
from God.

An Inner World

What is God's will?
I don't have
a clue.
What is more interesting
is God's imagination.
God imagined a universe
of infinite possibilities.

Out of God's glorious
imagination
evolved endless varieties
of unique animals.
A giraffe, an elephant,
a zebra, a lion,
a deer, a hippopotamus,
and the always entertaining
monkey.
There was also a wide world
of insects and rodents,
none of which I will mention.

In the sea, there emerged
countless varieties of fish.
And the sky was filled
with a wild and colorful
assortment of birds.

In time, along came
humans.
And each human
contained an
inner world of
endless possibilities . . .
most of which went
unexplored
as many of us prefer
safety, routine, and conformity.
We dare not live
our dreams . . . or realize
we can create alternate
possibilities for all of humanity.

PART FIVE

Scribbled Thoughts II

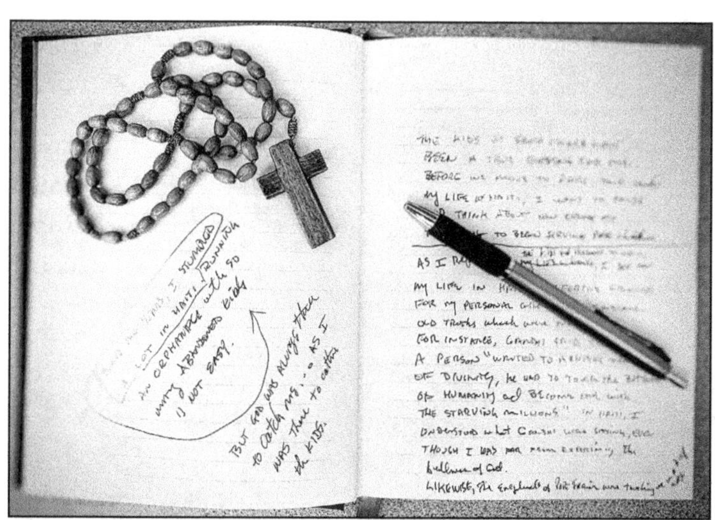

There is never any need
to dress up the truth.
Truth travels best unadorned.

The universe is clothed
in diversity,
yet humankind seeks
and religion claims
one truth.

Is it possible
to learn enough to
erase doubt?

The more informed
I become,
the more confused
I become.

If only for a day
I could take refuge
in the comfort of certainty.

Saw the following message
on a billboard
in front of a church:
"Faith sees things
that are out of sight.
To the believer,
that statement is profound;
to the unbeliever,
it is profoundly stupid."

The ability to reason
does not make a person
reasonable.

We humans want
to possess the truth,
yet it is only in
searching for truth
that we can expand
our abilities to be
more human,
more thoughtful,
more loving.

Unless your beliefs
have never been questioned,
or have hardened into
ritualistic dogma,
it is their nature to change
as you change
or your circumstances change.

The more I read of history,
the more I believe
that humans from
distant, past centuries
were not very different from us.
Progress has been painfully slow.

If you laid a heart and a brain
side by side on a table,
you couldn't help but reach
the conclusion that both organs
are rather repulsive looking,
and you could never reach
the conclusion that these two blobs
could cause so much trouble.

It seems clear to me
that passion,
not reason,
rules the world . . .
and our lives.
Life is laced with
inconsistencies
and contradictions.

Life is flux.

Life is filled with
ambiguity, failure, and false starts . . .
and that's OK.

Life is a school;
you keep learning
until graduation,
which comes at death.

Life throws things at you . . .
some good, some bad.

The path that does not challenge
is going in the wrong direction.

The future has no blueprint.
Anything can happen.

Everything that matters
is a mystery.

As we walk down
the path of life,
confrontations with

the inexplicable
lurk around
many a corner.

To live is to struggle,
day in and day out,
with all the foibles and failures
that are part of being human.

Within each of us
there is both longing
and limitation.

Life is a banquet;
sadly, most people
are starving.

Modern life has become
a dizzying merry-go-round
of nonstop activity
where it seems most of us
are doing a thousand things
all at once,
where people are
working longer hours and
whose lives are increasingly
fragmented by an
endless array of demands,
where multitasking and
instant messaging are the norm
in the consumer-crazed,
computer-driven,
cell phone crazy,
AI world of ours that has
virtually no room for
stillness and silence.

Fear is manufactured
in the brain;
love is born
in the heart.
Fear kills love.

Love exaggerates
the good in people.

Every life is
a long list of
remembered losses.

Life and death
breathe and expire
in seconds,
not years.

Life is mostly
failure.
Failure is not found
in falling down
but in not getting up.

An occasional dose of
novelty or nonsense
can act as a tonic
for the mind.

Encourage playfulness.

Laughter lightens the soul.

Sometimes I forget
how bad my memory is.

The mind needs no training
in how to destroy
through willful memory loss
whatever in its past
doesn't support
its present point of view.

Whatever you believe to be
true today,
you should be willing
to accept as
false tomorrow.

It is necessary for
one experience to die
so another
experience can be born.
Life is a series of deaths,
the disappearance of
values and ideas
that no longer serve.

So much of the crazy busyness
that consumes modern life
is an existential mask
that hides our inner emptiness.

While many people hunger
for truth,
society feeds us a steady diet
of trivia.

I used to enjoy
religious and spiritual debates.
No more.

Spiritual and religious
absolutism is arrogant,
dangerous, and
a roadblock to truth.

The path to truth
is paved by
personal and communal
experience and interpretation,
aided by sparks of insight
from our own personal stories
and the life stories
of members of our family,
friends, and communities.

I have no desire
to confront
or correct
anyone.
I want only
to confront
and correct
myself.

In the space of life's
darkest moments,
wisdom and light
begin to flow.

Idleness invigorates
the mind
and creates space
for inspiration.

To become vulnerable
and powerless is
to become totally
dependent upon God.

Faith requires
a passion
for the truth.

To live in
the reality of God
is to live in trust,
transparency, and compassion.
To live in
the reality of God
is to be embraced
by God's tenderness.

To know God
is not
to know fear.
To be a follower of Christ
is to celebrate
the tenderness of God.

The same tender mercy
that sustains me
sustains my enemy.

We often find it very difficult
to offer forgiveness.
Not so God; for God,
forgiveness is effortless.
In fact, God takes joy
in forgiveness
because it
generates new life.

Bring down
the barriers
within us
and between
other people.

When you encounter
the poor
—or any person—
you encounter
the Lord
and you are
changed.

In the furnace
of life,
our lives
are molded.

A leader is always
pointing people
to hope.

Hope comes from God.
Despair does not come from God.

The resurrection
is all about
hope.

When you are
Vulnerable,
there is room
for God.

The nearness of God
gradually dawned
on me.

I can't explain
my love
for all the kids
at SCCC.
But it is
real.

Kids are open
to miracles.

God experiences
pain.
God hurts.
His Son was
killed.

The Father experienced
the pain of
His Son's killing.

Christianity reflects
how broken
we are.

We need deep conviction
as well as humility.
Doubt is an important part
of faith.

God is relational.

Will the words
we speak
be pleasing to
the ears
of God?

Differences are not
a problem
that need to be
solved.

When you are keenly aware
of your own weakness,
your heart grows in mercy
for everyone, especially
the weak.

We have reduced Christ
to a sublime abstraction,
making it possible
to ignore
the very truth of Christ.

We all have
a secret
inner life.
This is what
makes us
humans . . .
and different from
all other forms
of life.

No two humans
are the same
thanks to the
amazingly different
internal worlds,
which sees things
vastly different.

No one has
experienced
what I have
experienced.
Just like you,
I am unique,
Because my
inner life is
uniquely mine.

My patterns
of thinking
must change
for me
to see
differently.

What we
exclude and
avoid
is what can
change us.

In the presence
of the one
you love
you begin
to see
who you really
are.

I want to live
the life
I imagine
so that when
I die
I will be pleased
that I lived
the life I loved.

Live the life
your heart
wants to live.

Santa Chiara
was simply
a possibility.
Slowly
with time
and work
and prayer
it became
a reality.

I have done
a lot of good
even though
I was not
always good.

Become the
artist
of your
life.

God gives you
the space
to be
who you are.

Monastery Musings

The following were written in October 2000 during a weeklong stay at Christ in the Desert monastery in New Mexico.

Seeking union with God
demands continual prayer.
Our lives must become
a continual prayer.

A quiet mind
and a peaceful soul
attune a person to hear
the voice of God.

Detachment reflects
the realization
that God alone matters.

What is necessary
is simple;
what is unnecessary
is complicated.

Our primary call
is to stand before God
in a stance of conversion.

Simplicity safeguards
the spirit from distractions
and leads it to God.

Stop measuring your progress.
In fact, let go
of the idea of "progress."

Prayer is hanging on
to God,
stubbornly clinging
to God.

Physical solitude is nothing
without an inner solitude.

Seek God
in the ordinary events
of daily life.

Solitude is
a presence,
not an absence.

Silence is
the soul of simplicity.

Simplicity is
the sister of purity.

Silence is
an expression
of love and strength.

Solitude gives you the ability
to hear an inner voice
longing to tell you
the truth about yourself.

Without voice,
God silently speaks
in and through everything.

Without silence,
we are deaf.

Our real pilgrimage
is into the depths of silence . . .
and leads to a true light.

The more I pray,
the deeper I enter
the darkness of the
absence of evidence.

Prayer deepens
with purification
of faults.

You grow into
what you
dwell upon.

The loud drumbeat of
fear and anxiety
can be quieted
by contemplation.

Contentment is
the daughter
of simplification.

Detachment makes
one powerful.

To keep silence
is to keep listening.

The only thing worth learning
is prayer.
Nothing else matters.

Washing the dishes
can be
an act of prayer.

Empty your heart;
sit in stillness.

Quiet your fears;
rest in God.

The desert is a place
of contemplation,
not discovery.

Punctuate your day
with thoughts of God,
recalling God's unselfish,
self-giving love for us.

Detachment reflects
the realization that
God alone matters.

Solitude allows the soul
to look upon everything
and see unity.

Prayer creates
a listening heart.

Prayer is
the breath of life.

Prayer acknowledges
our dependency
on God.

Prayer helps us
become more aware
of God's presence.

The goal of prayer is
communion with God.

Thoughts Scribbled on Merton's Table

In December 2000, I was graced with the rare opportunity to spend a week of solitude in Thomas Merton's hermitage in the woods on the grounds of the Cistercian Abbey of Gethsemani. When I was not wrestling with the silence, I made short notes of my thoughts and feeble insight into the monk's life. My book Reading Thomas Merton and Longing for God in Haiti *excavates my interest in Merton and my desire to follow St. Francis of Assisi deeper in the pain of severe poverty found in the slums of the world on periphery of life.*

An artist who works
out of certainty
is cooked.

Mysticism is
at its core
a conscious intimacy
of intercourse
between God
and humanity.

Look for "moments" of prayer.

Growth in purity
is linked to increasing
our ability to
establish and maintain
solitude of soul
for God alone.

Through simplicity
we learn that self-denial
paradoxically leads to
true self-fulfillment.

Simplicity allows us
to hold the interests of others
above our self-interest.
Real simplicity is
true freedom.

It is in stillness
that we find
our emptiness,
the emptiness
that can only be filled
by welcoming God
into our hearts.

Sex, power, fame,
and money
are not enough
to still the longing
within us.
Only God
is enough.

If you greet sunrise with
God in your heart
and a prayer on your lips,
your day stands a better chance
of reflecting God's love,
mercy, and justice,
and you will be better able
to treat others the way God would.

Voluntary physical poverty
is a means to
a healthy spiritual poverty.

Exterior and interior
poverty are close friends.

A spirit of poverty
makes detachment from
possessions possible.
Poverty of spirit fights
the instinct to possess.

Gratification of the instinct
to possess material things
makes one susceptible to
the vice of selfishness—
grabbing all you can for yourself,
without regard for others.

Poverty and charity
are soulmates.

Poverty brings you
closer to Christ.

Our possessions should be used
to sustain life.
We have a right to possess
whatever we need
to sustain life.
But we do not have a right
to acquire more and more possessions
just to satisfy a need to possess,
to accumulate more and more things.

Monastic life is
a way of self-emptying.

Self-abandonment is a
continual forgetting
of one's self
to constantly remember
God.

We have forgotten the Cross.
But the crucifixion of Christ
cannot be reversed.
Paradise has been paved over;
happiness on earth is impossible—
without the Cross, without God.

Surrender is never easy.
When Jesus was called
to his final surrender
on the cross,
he sweat blood.

Happiness is being happy
with what you have.

The mystery of life
cannot be solved
with scientific
or psychological
answers.
The key to the solution,
if there even is one,
is mystical.

"Surrender" is a positive word
in the language of spirituality.
It allows us to receive
the gift of new life
in God's saving action.

I'm stunned by how often
in my life
I have failed to see
the difference between
what is real and
what is superficial.

Solitude is the womb
of discernment.

Jesus did what
he had to do
on the cross.
Now it is our turn,
our turn to surrender
completely.

As the richness of
poverty of spirit
increases,
petty thoughts, cares,
and anxieties diminish.

I overlook
more often
than I look.

God's will
for each of us
is that we live
lives of unselfish
charity.

We need to find
ourselves
and give ourselves
away.

God seeks intimacy.

God's love
does not shout,
it whispers.

God has chosen
to be vulnerable
and defenseless.
Jesus was as helpless
as we are,
for he was
"like us in all things but sin."
He was unprotected
and unprivileged.

I am poor, needy,
and helpless—thank God!

I would never
deliberately choose
self over God—
except that I do so
in countless little ways
every day without realizing it.

God is not asking us
to become perfect;
God is asking us
to surrender everything.

God wants us
to give up
our illusions.
We hate this.
We like pretending
that good is
within our reach.

Every day, God comes
to us in human form—
and we turn our back.

Prayer is hard
because it demands
honesty before God.

Life is full of delicate shadings,
of contrasts,
of sunlight and shadow;
it is a constant play
of opposites.

Thoughts Scribbled While Walking the Streets of Kensington

Kensington was a deeply impoverished section of Philadelphia where I made two films about the St. Francis Inn, a soup kitchen operated by Franciscan friars.

To be in communion with
those who are suffering
is the surest way to chip away
at the notion you are
a separate self,
detached from
the rest of creation.

Letting go of
my life
is the surest way
to a life
of abundance.

The kingdom of God
is about relationships
manifesting compassion
and forgiveness
and producing peace and justice.

Eternal life is
not something that
happens in the future:
It is now.

The Communion of Saints

Artist credit: Barbara Carr

Social Mystics

The Hebrew prophets
are mystically united
with St. Francis of Assisi
along with the sages
of all religions
who felt the pain
of the impoverished
and the disenfranchised.

Today, the global struggle
for dignity and human rights
finds people with
deep experiences of faith
longing to see society
transformed.
Our personal spiritual journey
must evolve into the
global sphere.

Personal mysticism grows
into social mysticism
that reaches out
to the oppressed.
We are one.
No one is left out.

The communion of saints
who embodied
mystic-activism include
Mahatma Gandhi,
Martin Luther King, Jr.,
Abraham Joshua Heschel,

Thich Nhat Hanh,
Dorothy Day,
and Thomas Merton.

Their personal prayer life
gave birth to a firm resolve
to make a difference
through an expression
of excessive love
of all creation.
For them
action and contemplation
were not distinct and separate
aspects of the spiritual life,
but one and the same,
united to make
profound changes.

Liberation should not be
focused solely on a
heavenly afterlife,
but needs to address
inequality within
the cultural forces
that imprison
people: poverty,
war, colonialism,
and the displacement
of millions of people
due to war, famine,
dictators, and
climate change.

Poverty, segregation,
and hunger
strip people of
their inherent dignity
and extinguish hope.

The fullness of life
that God wishes
for all people
is thwarted by
all these social iniquities.
We must actively
unite and work at
removing the
social and political obstacles
that prevent many people
from experiencing
the fullness of life
God wishes for them.

We need to foster
an ever-deepening
spirit of compassion.
We need to
speak and act
nonviolently.
We need to
stand up
for those who are
forced down.

With hearts
united in peace and
altruistic love
the world torn apart

by war, tyranny, and injustice
can be changed into
a paradisical garden
of harmony for all.

Sadly, spiritual fractures
are ripping apart
the soul of humanity.

After sitting in prayerful silence,
we need to stand up and
feed the hungry,
comfort the hurting,
inspire the hopeless,
and oppose all forms
of injustice and prejudice,
as well as advocate for
the spiritual unity of the
sacred and secular
through intercultural
and interreligious
dialogue.

After abandoning
in my twenties
the Catholic faith
passed onto to me
by virtue of my birth
and subsequent return
to Christianity
thirty years ago,
I slowly came to see that
Christian theology is
a blank daybook
where the story
of my own life

can be intertwined
with the stories
of all the saints,
prophets, and disciples
who desired
to wholeheartedly
follow Jesus.
I am also
spiritually lifted up
by the inspirational
and universal mystics
born into other faiths.

It is seeing
the Oneness of life
that gives birth to
compassion, generosity,
and hope.
Life is One.
Dualism is
a deception.
There is no separation
between the spiritual
and the material realms.
Anything that

separates and divides us
is incompatible with the
reality of God.

The entire world
is one family,
consisting of
animals, humans,
flowers, rivers,
and all of creation
united in God
and caring for
each other.
Interdependence
is a big word
that encapsulates
the entire world
as a family.
Everything depends upon
everything else.

There is no me
without you
and You.

No matter the faith
each of us holds
to be true—
for oneself, at least—
it is our sacred duty
to stand in solidarity
with any form of
oppression
wherever it is found.

God Is at Home Among the Poor

Tuesday, January 18, 2013—10:30 p.m.

I am flying over Guadalajara, Mexico [on my way to Honduras], which sends my mind flying back to the long days I filmed in Mexico while making *Endless Exodus*. I thought about my friend Brother Ed Dunn, OFM. I spent a few days with him in Cabo San Lucas . . . which sounds like fun, but believe me fun it was not; Br. Ed lived in an inland barrio occupied by poor migrants trying to eke out a living working in menial jobs at the lush resorts. Most cannot make ends meet and are forced to head for the States and the deadly trip across the desert. These barrios are nightmares, a blight on society. People live without running water and with stolen electricity in homes made of cardboard and scrap wood. Here are a few scraps of my narration from the film:

We betray Jesus when
for the sake of expediency,
we are willing to sacrifice justice
and turn our backs on the poor.

When we make space
for the newcomer,
the alien,
we make space
for the son of God
to be born again.
Hospitality is
the secret to unlocking
the mystery of the Incarnation.

It seems inevitable
that some people
will get jobs in Cabo,
and some won't,

that some will get water and
     electricity,
and some won't,
that some people will get across
     the border
and find a decent job in the
     United States,
and some won't.
But the Incarnation pushes us
to distrust the inevitable
and to work for a society
in which there is space for all,
in which there is enough
food, water, and electricity for all.

Christ is born again
in this dusty barrio
in Cabo San Lucas
where the new chapel being built

[a hurricane blew the old one
    away]
is a sign that the only inevitable
    virtue
is the one of hope.

I'm slowly learning to see myself
in the migrants.
We are all migrants.
We are all poor.
I need to reject the false security
    I seek
and accept my inability
to control the future.
Christ asks for conversion every
    day,
that every day we surrender more
    of ourselves
to the all-embracing love of God.
This is hard, very hard indeed.
But it's the border we must cross
to find a better life . . . in God.

During my time in Cabo San
    Lucas,
I stayed with four [Franciscan]
    friars
who serve the poor . . .
and learn from the poor.

For the poor, faith in God
is their most prized possession.
They trust God for everything
while caring for each other.

The poor help me
unmask my own poverty.
Still, I want to deny my poverty,
but the poor give me
the hope and courage to face it.

In the face and presence
of the poor
we can learn to see
the face and presence
of Christ.

God is at home
among the poor.
Jesus was born amid
their poverty and rejection.

Like the poor and oppressed,
Jesus was despised and rejected.
Like the poor and oppressed,
Jesus was hungry and
    discouraged.
Jesus did not come
as a royal ruler,
as king of the universe.
He was born into poverty
and lived among the poor.
He was an outcast,
living among outcasts,
living among people
with no privilege or rights.

His message was so radical,
so unsettling,

he was quickly put to death
for threatening to turn
the established power structure
upside down.

Poverty gives birth
to hunger and despair.
Poverty means

one bad thing
after another. Worse,
poverty often also means
death.

Death by poverty
blasphemes the reign of life
proclaimed by Christ.

We need to transform
borders
into
thresholds.

God is an artist of exodus.

Note: Brother Ed Dunn, OFM, died on February 12, 2006, at Mission San Luis Rey in Oceanside, California. He was a dear friend. I was at his bedside in the friary the moment he passed. With me was a Franciscan friar from Ireland who had lived with Ed in El Salvador. The Irish friar was in California to attend some meetings with me. We were supposed to visit him on February 13th, but when some time opened on the 12th, I told the Irish friar I had a feeling we needed to visit Ed right away. When we arrived, Ed was unconscious. He was surrounded by family and friars. They were all exhausted. Our presence gave them a chance to take a break. The Irish friar and I read psalms to Ed as he slipped away. Some say he was hanging on, waiting for our visit. Brother Ed was one of my many teachers on living the Franciscan Charism. Ed was just over a month short of his 57th birthday.

Becoming Less than Zero

While filming the poor and living with the poor, I discovered a wisdom that can only be learned by living the Gospel in a radical way. Seeing, feeling, and experiencing the reality of those barely living on the peripheries of life is where I awoke to deeper reality and a more intense encounter with the living God.

To waste your life
on trivialities is
to become trivial.

No one wants to be
trivial.
Yet most of us are
active participants in the
trivialization of humanity.
Jesus pointed us toward the
divinization of humanity.

Jesus would not be on
Tweeter or Facebook
or any other
social media platform.
Nor Netflix
or any crap coming from
Hollywood.
Television is a weapon
of mass distraction,
distracting us
from reality
and helping us
ignore the unjust,
unnecessary suffering
of most of humanity.

Jesus would be
down in the gutter with
the lost, lonely, rejected,
despised, and abandoned . . .
offering all a helping hand
and an embrace of mercy.

Unplug all social media,
all forms of entertainment,
and see, feel, and experience
the reality of those barely living
on the peripheries of life . . .
where you will find the poor
and Christ in rags.
If you do unplug
from the digitized unreality,
you will be amazed at
the transformation
of your life.

Of course, this will take
more courage and faith
than you imagine you have.
But this is the beauty,
    the miracle.

By decreasing the many things
you now cherish,
the addiction will weaken,
and you will be awakened to
a new reality,
and, in time, encounter
the boundless love and mercy
of God . . .
not empty words
about God.

Slowly, you will grow
in humility,
in meekness,
in holiness.

You might have, in time,
the wings of an angel,
the voice of a prophet,
the sanctity of a saint.

But those are not our goals.
We want to reach the zenith
of whatever we do.
Christ would become
less than zero.

By emptying ourselves,
by becoming zero,
we will be free for
a fuller encounter
with the living God.

The Miracle of Santa Chiara

In May 2025, I quietly commemorated the tenth anniversary of the founding of the Santa Chiara Children's Center in Port-au-Prince, Haiti, in May 2015. As I thought about this improbable milestone, I was inspired to write a poem that captured my feelings as I sat in exile in Florida, far from the home in Haiti that I love.

The Santa Chiara
Children's Center
was made
by, through, and with
pain . . .
to relieve the pain
of broken kids
in hopes of
healing them,
making them
whole.

The kids arrived
at our gate
cast off,
abandoned,
lost.
They were hungry
for food
and love.

Life had left them
withered,
weathered,
weakened . . .
and wounded

in mind and heart.
Some were
skin and bones.
Some had been
abused and beaten.
Yet, they were
chosen by us
to receive
from our hands
the tender care
they deserved
as children of God.

Over the last
ten years
we carried
each other's pain.
We went from
crisis to crisis
with a silent prayer
in our hearts.
We were surrounded
by violence
but stayed
focused on
peaceful coexistence.

We were always
on the edge of
extinction,
on the verge of
bankruptcy.
Yet, funds
kept coming,
even if at
the last second.

We were often
nagged by
doubts
yet never lost
faith.
We often
quivered with
fear
but never lost
hope.

I look back

Lord Jesus Christ,
Son of God,
have mercy
on me,
a sinner.

in amazement at
the miracle
that is the
Santa Chiara
Children's Center.
Through ten years of
pain and struggle,
it has become
—against all odds—
a home of hope
and healing.

Santa Chiara is
an island of
peace and harmony
in sea of
chaos and violence.
It is a place
of transformation
where God's love
can be seen, felt,
and shared.

The Bottom Rung

We are in a time of
    upheaval and horror.
So much is wrong.
So many injustices.
Democracy is dying.
Dictatorships are spreading.
    Distress and despair
    fear and angst
fill the air. We seem lost
    for answers, a way out
    of the insanity.
Faith and hope are hard
    to hold on to during
    so much uncertainty.

My recent time of
contemplative solitude
in forests of the Berkshires
filled my heart
    with hope and
    with a desire
to be in the heart of
    human suffering,
to be a helping hand
in transfiguring
    that suffering.

I cannot go to Haiti.
But I can attune myself
    to the suffering
    of others
wherever I am.

Prayer prompts me
to reach out
in compassion to
the suffering and weak,
and helps me embrace
all of humanity.

In prayer,
I learn what to do,
how to respond to the poor,
the persecuted, and the
    suffering.
And it is prayer
that sustains and guides
what I try do for them,
no matter how often I fail.

Over the last twenty-five years
I have learned that
    following Jesus
requires daily self-sacrifice
and shattering most
    of my personal goals
and plans.
Goodbye penthouse in
    Hollywood.
Hello slum in Haiti.
Downward mobility
became the way up
to a higher consciousness
    of God.

The sixth-century Orthodox
    monk
St. John Climacus
wrote "The Ladder of Divine
    Ascent"
in which he addresses
asceticism and spirituality.
He used the metaphor of a ladder
with thirty rungs
to symbolize the journey of
spiritual growth,
urging readers to ascend from
earthly concerns
toward Divine union.
Using the saint's metaphor,
I am still on the
    bottom rung.

May God Give You Peace

About the Author

Gerard Thomas Straub had a long and distinguished career as a network television producer and executive in New York and Hollywood; he produced dramatic series that have aired on CBS, NBC, and ABC. He went on to write and direct over 20 documentary films focusing on the plight of the poor in such poverty-stricken nations as India, Kenya, Uganda, Jamaica, Haiti, Brazil, Peru, Honduras, El Salvador, Mexico, and The Philippines.

Mr. Straub is the author of twelve books. *The Sun & Moon Over Assisi* was named the "Best Spirituality Hardcover Book of the Year" in 2001 by the Catholic Press Association. *The Loneliness and Longing of Saint Francis* was a 2015 winner in the Spirituality category of the Association of Catholic Publishers' "Excellence in Publishing Awards."

Gerry also taught a course on television writing and directing at the Pontifical Gregorian University in Rome, Italy. He has spoken at more than 260 Catholic churches, high schools, and universities across the U.S., as well as in Canada, France, Italy, and Hungary. He has been awarded three honorary doctorate degrees in recognition of his work on behalf of the poor.

Gerry lives primarily in Port-au-Prince, Haiti where he operates the Santa Chiara Children's Center, a home for forty-five abandoned and displaced kids. He has a small apartment in Vero Beach, Florida.